The Engagement Ring Guide for Men

Khordipour and Shaddaie

Copyright © 2019 by Khordipour and Shaddaie
All rights reserved.

No part of this publication may be reproduced, distributed or transmitted in any form or by any means, including photocopying, recording or other electronic or mechanical methods, without the prior written permission of the publisher, except in the case of brief quotations embodied in reviews and certain other non-commercial uses permitted by copyright law.

For permission requests please contact Canoe Tree Press.

Published 2019

Printed in the United States of America
Print ISBN: 978-1-951490-30-0

Canoe Tree Press
4697 Main Street
Manchester, VT 05255

www.CanoeTreePress.com

CONTENT

Introduction 5
Chapter 1 - Are You Ready to Propose? 9
Chapter 2 - Discovering Her Style 39
Chapter 3 - A Guide to Engagement Rings 75
Chapter 4 - How to Propose 115
Chapter 5 - Caring for your Engagement Ring 139
Chapter 6 - What Else You Should Know 165
About Us 205

INTRODUCTION

WHO IS THIS BOOK FOR?

Since you picked up this book, I'm guessing that you're somewhere in the more serious stages of your relationship. If so, this book was written for you. But if you don't fall into this category, don't feel left out just yet. Even if you are already married (and have an engagement ring), I would still strongly recommend reading on. There is so much more to this book than just tips on proposing.

We chose to address this book to guys in their 20s, 30s, and 40s as they seem to be the ones who could use this information most, and we want them to feel armed with information before making one of the largest purchases of their life.

That being said, this book is by no means limited to this demographic. All ages can enjoy this book and take valuable lessons from it. We showed this manuscript to so many test readers from various backgrounds and many of them loved the book. The reactions were almost always the same — shock. Most of them had never heard of half the things in this book! Even our friends within the jewelry industry discovered lots of things they never knew before.

WHY WE WROTE THIS BOOK

We saw a desperate need for our book. It's really that simple.

We've been selling vintage rings and jewelry for 40 years, and although we strive to educate our customers throughout the buying process, we noticed a big problem: most guys who are looking to buy jewelry enter the store with almost no prior knowledge. It's almost as if they're trying to drive from the backseat, and as a result they were completely at the mercy of the jeweler.

Customers usually come into our showroom (or email and call us) with a few jewelry keywords in their pocket — and that's it. All the other jewelry knowledge, much of which being very important to the purchase, is completely foreign to them.

Most guys don't even know what the word "carat" actually means. Important words like filigree, triple-wire, bezel, milgrain, or polished girdle are like a different language to them.

It's something that has bothered us for years. Last year, however, we decided that we were going to fix this problem. We set out to write a book that would provide guys with all the answers that they would need to know before buying their engagement ring.

As we began writing, we realized that we have a lot more to share than just jewelry information, and so we expanded the book to cover a lot more. Over the years we've had the honor of having a front-row seat to thousands of wedding proposals, and there was so much that we needed to share.

Here is what you can expect to learn from our book:

- Diamond Education
- Jewelry Education
- Tips to Saving Money
- How to Propose
- Engagement Ring Customs and Traditions

INTRODUCTION

- Discovering her Style (without asking)
- Are you Ready to get Married?

OUR PREFERENCE TOWARDS VINTAGE

As you read this book, you will notice our strong preference towards vintage jewelry. We believe that vintage jewelry is far superior to modern jewelry.

It is important to note, however, that this book is not only useful for couples looking to buy a vintage ring. Anyone ready to buy any type of engagement ring will be able to use this book to its full potential.

ABOUT US

Michael Khordipour and Afshin Shaddaie founded Estate Diamond Jewelry in 1980. We started our company with a common love for rare and old jewelry, realizing that there was a market of like-minded people who wanted something special and unique for their wedding proposal, and so we threw our energy into vintage and custom-made rings.

Before long we became the world's top authority on vintage rings. Collectors, celebrities, and royalty began making appointments to view our collections at our 5th Avenue showroom. Our company quickly generated international attention.

Recently, Michael's son Benjamin joined the company and Afshin and Benjamin decided that it was high time to put this book in motion.

Writing this book has taken almost a year, but it has been a wonderful experience.

We would love to hear how this book helped you. Please feel free to leave us a message at www.estatediamondjewelry.com/book

CHAPTER 1
ARE YOU READY TO PROPOSE?

Love, when it's strong and healthy, doesn't only make you feel great, it inspires you to act. If you are in love and she is in love, then you are probably as ready as you could ever be to propose.

Still, take a deep breath. Let your feelings settle for a moment. Look at all the other things that matter in a relationship, the big and the small, too.

Consider now the state of your relationship. Are you on the verge of bliss? Do you only have to flutter your wings a little to reach her?

ARE YOU REALLY READY FOR MARRIAGE?

If you pop the question before you're both ready, it can result in an uncomfortable situation and potentially lead to doubts and hesitations that you could have avoided if you had timed your proposal right.

The question should be largely symbolic. Certainly, the answer could still be no, but the real purpose of proposing is for both of you to show that you choose one another.

The best thing you can do at this stage is to leave the questions and doubts and focus on what the two of you have created so far. Draw strength and confidence from all the happy moments you've shared and you'll know you're moving in the right direction.

No one can tell you if you're ready to propose or not. That's entirely up to you. But there are some signs that you may be ready. Here are some telltale hints that you've found the right person and that it's the right time to take that big step.

You've Reached a Stable Place in Your Life

Unions in which one or both people are looking for the other person to fill in a missing piece of themselves can be challenging. All the insecurities that you bring into a marriage will surface and affect the relationship sooner or later.

The fact is that marriage means making a little room in your life for another person. For some people, the feeling that they haven't had a chance to live their own life can seriously jeopardize a marriage. When you are satisfied and you know that you've experienced the world on your own terms, you'll know you're ready to start experiencing it with someone else.

If you still feel apprehension about the experiences that you won't be having anymore after proposing, that's a problem. In behaviorist terms, that's called FOMO — fear of missing out — and it's a downward spiral that inevitably leads to resentment. When you're with the right person, you won't think too hard about the other things you're not doing because you'll be content with her. This isn't to say that you'll never want to spend time apart but, when it comes down to it, quality time together should beat most of the alternatives.

There's a physiological aspect to this as well. The decision making and planning part of our brains develops very slowly and only begins to mature around the age of 22. Not that there's a perfect age to propose, because there isn't, but there is a level of maturity that will make a successful marriage much more likely. To know what that is, you have to be completely honest with yourself about who you are and how far you've come. You wouldn't want to play a game of cards with an incomplete deck, so don't make major life decisions without a fully-developed sense of self.

It's also useful to have experienced a degree of independence in your life before you commit to a marriage. This means different things to different people but, generally speaking, you should have lived on your own or with roommates, experienced financial independence, and spent time being single.

Exceptions to this rule include high school and college sweethearts. If you found your soul mate at an early stage in your life, you're luckier than you know. The percentage of people who marry their first love is in the single digits. Among those lucky few, the most successful are the ones who wait until their mid-20s to marry. So even if you do find "the one," you'll have much better odds of staying together if you give yourselves time to grow into your own skin.

Unless there is an urgent reason to get married early, it may be in your best interest to give it some time. Don't think of it as a trial period for the person you're with. Instead, think of it as giving your relationship a chance to blossom naturally and find out how it fits into your plans for the future.

The Honeymoon Phase Has Long Passed

As humans, we crave novelty, and the novelty of the beginning of a relationship is often a period of deep infatuation where everything seems possible. This "honeymoon phase" generally lasts for a year or two, depending on the couple. When that intoxicating feeling starts to wear off and the routines of life take over is when the real nature and potential of a relationship begin to show.

It's easy to mistake the honeymoon phase for the truest form of love and experience dismay when it starts wearing off. The sad reality is that this person you were so enchanted with when you first met will become a stable and predictable part of your life. It's all too common to mistake that feeling of familiarity with a sense of boredom. Instead, you should see it as the natural progression of the relationship, one that opens many new avenues for your love to grow and expand.

When the honeymoon phase ends, the vibrancy and excitement that blinded you will clear up and you'll see that the person you love is very different from what you initially imagined. This isn't necessarily a bad thing. If you can navigate this transition correctly, that's a very good sign that the relationship has what it takes to transform into a solid marriage. In a perfect world, you'll begin to do a few things differently.

You'll both begin to rely on each other more than you have before. In managing your differences, you'll start to clearly see how much you need them by your side — and, you will begin to see the ways in which she relies on you. This isn't only limited to physical things, because in close relationships partners tend to distribute mental processes and make better decisions together.

As a couple, there is no doubt that you will both disappoint and excite one another from time to time, creating an emotional economy. This is a staple of long-term relationships that either strengthens the bond or dissolves it. If you've been together for a while, it's plainly strengthening.

A key landmark of the honeymoon phase giving way to a more durable relationship is when other people start mattering as much as they used to before your relationship. In the early stages of a relationship, it's easy to fall into the habit of neglecting your inner circle of friends and family. When you both start to let other people take more prominent roles in your lives again, you'll know you're on the right track. This will often lead to demands and expectations that might strain the relationship, but if the foundation is solid, that will serve as a rallying point rather than the start of a crack in the fabric of your bond.

People often make the mistake of panicking when the honeymoon phase starts to decline. This can lead to a series of poor decisions to try to reignite the passion that was once felt. A hasty proposal is one of the biggest and the most common mistakes. Proposing just to get back to that blissful place is a recipe for disaster because it adds a layer of expectation that only further strains the entire relationship. Instead, the proposal should come after the honeymoon phase is over and the relationship has evolved into something bigger and more stable.

Ultimately, marriage allows most couples to experience a second honeymoon phase, which is something to look forward to. This time around, however, you're a little older — and hopefully wiser — so the decline will be much less strenuous.

Your Finances Are in Order

One of the biggest causes of strife in relationships is money. You should be honest about where you stand financially and expect the same from her. You don't have to be exceptionally wealthy, and if she considers it a qualifying condition, it may be worth reconsidering your commitment and your proposal.

However, you should be able to provide for yourself and, if you're intending to start a family, have a decent financial plan for how you're going to manage it. You should also have at least something along the lines of an emergency fund. This means that major purchases will have to be put off in favor of building up some savings. Also, you should start working towards getting a grip on impulse spending.

More importantly, it's something that you've discussed together before. Be open about any debt you have, and what your long term financial goals are. You should at least start to make preliminary plans together and discuss what standard of living you both find acceptable. If there are significant discrepancies between your plans and expectations, it could become a point of serious contention in the future.

This kind of conversation can be awkward, even for couples. People don't often discuss money in their daily lives but it's crucial to have an open discussion that will continue to exist throughout the eventual marriage. Talks of this sort should not be limited to debt. Current and future expected income, spending habits, and major expenses should all be discussed in as much detail as possible.

If you spend a lot of time with a person, many things will be revealed in due course. If one of you spends excessive amounts of money on impulse buys, it's hardly something that's going to be a secret. So, before you talk about this, you should do some preliminary research and consider your own spending habits. This way, once the cards are on the table you can zero in on specific issues that you find troubling.

There's no reason to make it a "gotcha" type of conversation, though. At some point, bring it up and let her know that it's something you want to discuss. You should both understand that it's going to be a little awkward, but if you communicate clearly and understand that you're working together, this might strengthen your current relationship and future marriage.

Proposing also figures into this in a big way. If you're considering proposing, you're setting yourself up for at least two big expenses. There's a potential third big expense, depending on how you choose to propose to your girlfriend.

The first is, of course, the engagement ring. The old two-months-salary rule is not a great guide. We'll get into the intricacies of how to figure out how much to spend later on in this book, but the fact remains that it's going to be a significant purchase. And while it's not a good solution for everyone, you might even choose to finance a ring.

The other large expense is going to be the wedding. In this case you'll probably have a lot of help from both of your families. However, know that it will make a dent in your bank account. Most people underestimate the cost of a wedding and reception.

The third potential expense is the honeymoon. Many couples choose to forego or postpone the honeymoon in order to save some money, and this may be something that actually works for you. But if you're one of those couples who want to go on a honeymoon straight away, it's yet another expense that needs to be planned for.

All in all, starting a life with another person takes a lot of planning and openness, especially when it comes to financial concerns.

Conflicts Are Addressed and Resolved Constructively

It's a given that conflicts will happen in relationships. They don't just happen in romantic relationships; give any interpersonal relation enough time and a conflict will inevitably occur. The key to having a lasting relationship is in knowing how to manage a conflict and resolve it in a constructive way that doesn't generate more conflicts in the future. If you don't learn to solve problems constructively in a reasonable amount of time, the problem will only get worse after marriage. Therefore, it should be seriously addressed before you consider moving on to that stage.

Ideally, romantic relationships should be seen as a system of equal exchange. Both parties are looking to get their needs met and when one side feels like they're giving more than they're getting, it naturally leads to conflict. An important thing to remember is that this sense of inequity stems from perceived notions of how you're giving and receiving love. It's not about getting affection or love in general, but rather getting the right kinds and getting them in the right way.

Conflict isn't an inherently negative thing or destructive force. If it's viewed and approached in a constructive way, it can serve as a catalyst to improve the relationship. That's the kind of conflict resolution you should aim to establish with her before you consider proposing.

Look at every conflict as an information gathering exercise — a way to learn about the shortcomings in the relationship from both sides. When approached like this, conflicts can be separated from the relationship and help the couple join forces to resolve them. Overcoming obstacles together strengthens the bond you have.

The real challenge lies in being able to re-frame arguments in this light whenever they arise. Sometimes it's hard to see how you could ever agree on a certain issue, and it in turn continues to remain basically unresolved. This is especially true during periods of high conflict, such as a long time spent apart or entering a new phase in your lives.

If there is no conflict whatsoever, it's usually a sign that the relationship lacks communication. These issues can be dismissed but they don't go away. If there's no avenue to communicate what bothers you, it's easy to start feeling powerless and unhappy in a relationship.

While healthy in the right context and the right amount, excessive conflicts can be a sign of trouble as well. If arguments about the same old issues and situations are cropping up consistently, it means that the problem in question hasn't been resolved. If the conflicts don't end with constructive and mutually beneficial solutions, it's hard to make such a relationship last. This doesn't always mean the gap between you can't be bridged, it just may mean that you don't have the skillset to argue effectively.

So how much is too much? It really depends. Some people are

significantly more conflict-averse than others and their tolerance for argument is very low. Other people seem more comfortable with arguing if it leads to some sort of constructive outcome. Whatever the case may be, the goal should always be to keep the relationship in perspective and avoid harboring resentment.

Here's a basic checklist to see whether your disagreements are healthy or not:

- They don't last longer than necessary
- They don't spill over to broader issues
- They don't spiral into personal attacks that bring up previous disappointments
- You are at least partly satisfied once they're over

If you've got all or most of those covered, you're addressing your conflicts constructively.

Friends and Family Think You're Right for Each Other

It's hard to overstate how important it is that the person you want to marry fits into your tribe. Our friends and family often see us more clearly than we see ourselves, and the fact that they're standing on the outside gives them a different, wider perspective. If you want your family to remain in your life after marriage, their approval is a big deal.

An important exception is if the people in your life are being deliberately obtuse and refuse to see things from the standpoint of your long-term well-being. They don't have to be thrilled about your partner, but they should at least support your union.

Think of it as a support system building for your relationship. It may not seem like a big deal, but having people to rely on in your life matters a lot. If you give up on those people, you'll need to find others to take their place or you run the danger of placing too much expectation on the relationship.

Also, going back to a previous point, if the people who care about you the most tell you that something's wrong, you should listen. You should at least take their advice seriously and try to be unbiased about what they're telling you. Keep in mind that they probably have your best interests in mind, so there's no reason to be defensive. If they have a wrong perception or if they've understood something the wrong way, you should speak with them and get to the bottom of their concerns.

Maintaining relationships with people whom you have to keep apart from each other is exhausting and it will end up hurting all sides. Moreover, knowing that they don't accept her, she's likely to become resentful of your family, which will cause even more strife. Inevitably, this type of conflict will make family gatherings awkward and they might become even more complicated when the children arrive.

Your friends and family may not be able to give you specific reasons why they dislike her, which makes everything that much harder. In that case, maybe they just haven't had the chance to get to know her well. The good news is that some quality time together can fix that. It's okay to ultimately decide that your relationship is more important, but not before you've made an honest effort to make it work.

Of course, this is all contingent on you having a healthy relationship with your family. But your close friends are just as important in your life.

On the flip side is another consideration. If her family doesn't like you, it's not something that should be taken lightly. In the long run, it will cause the same kind of problems for your relationship. If the love is there, you can probably work through those problems along the way, but it's easier to nip them in the bud. Make an effort to find out what it is about you that doesn't sit well with them and, if possible, engage them in a way that disproves their fears.

Staying together in a hostile social environment is very difficult and it can easily wear you both down. It's a point that will never be truly resolved unless it's handled early on. Being on good terms with each other's family and social circle is great evidence that the relationship is meant to last. Likewise, it's one more sign that you're ready to propose.

You've Been Through Some Highs and Lows

Nothing brings people together like overcoming shared adversity. It gives us a chance to see what we're made of and how much we can trust other people. In a relationship, this often means having someone who's there for you through the hard times and rainy days. Be that the loss of a loved one, losing your job, or any other major challenge.

Every time a couple goes through a stressful situation it either makes the couple stronger or erodes the bond between them. If you're with the right person, trials and tribulations will always make you stronger in the end.

The ideal relationship is one in which you help each other through challenges. If you feel like the relationship is only adding to the stress of life, it's a possible sign that it won't work. However, simply not adding more stress is not enough — a good partner will understand how to support you, help you work through the problems, and minimize your stress.

As human beings, we grow and change throughout our lives. It's inevitable that we will be exposed to new sources of stress as our circumstances change. Some of the problems we face are going to be out of our control, but it's important to recognize and accept them when they appear. These changes are especially prominent for couples because they involve two people growing in relation to each other, as well as the world. In a healthy relationship these changes will come and go, but as long as the foundation is strong, they shouldn't be a destabilizing force.

Sometimes, people fear that all changes are bad and find themselves longing to return to a previous stage of the relationship. This isn't only impossible, it's also wrong. Change is a key part of a relationship and it can't survive if it doesn't evolve over time. Though it may seem disheartening to take two steps forward and three steps back, that's how healthy relationships work. They change and evolve. The kind of relationship you can rely on in the long run is the one that can face and weather the storm, and stays strong in the process.

If you see these traits in your relationship, marriage will only strengthen your bond. It will just be another stepping stone along the road to a better understanding and happier life together. You can confidently take that next step.

You're Happy With Who She Is Now

As much as change is inevitable, you should also be happy with the person you are with now. That doesn't mean you should think she is perfect, but if you're hoping that she'll become someone else when you get married, you're setting yourself up for a huge disappointment. Getting engaged — and ultimately married — isn't going to change who she is, and that shouldn't be your goal.

If you fell in love with her, there's clearly something there, even if she's not exactly the way you initially envisioned her. Harboring feelings of dissatisfaction is only going to make things harder in the long run. Instead, focus on the things that made you fall in love with her in the first place. You may eventually find that there really isn't enough there, but don't think that marriage will change her and make her more to your liking.

Many times, things that you don't like about her will have a lot to do with things you need to fix about yourself. These kinds of relationship problems can be hard to recognize and own up to, but don't fall into the trap of mistaking your own shortcomings for hers.

Another pitfall is focusing on changing your partner instead of dealing with other, deeper issues in the relationship. If you're an affectionate person and she doesn't like grand displays of affection, that's not something she has to change. It's a foundational element of the relationship that isn't working. The solution isn't to try to make her more affectionate. Instead, try to reach a healthy compromise through dialogue or come to terms with the fact that it may not work out in the long run. If you keep insisting on changing her, it can stifle communication between you and prevent you from solving the problem in a mutually beneficial way.

You may also be holding on to certain expectations that have no place in a mature relationship. There's only so much another person can do for you, especially as you start to take on more responsibilities in your lives. How satisfied you are in your relationship and your life in general largely depends on your expectations. A shift in perspective may do more for your relationship and your overall well-being than any potential change in your partner.

Of course, there are also things that your partner will do wrong, things that you're legitimately going to be upset about. In such cases, holding on to things you want to change in them will only exacerbate the frustration you feel.

That's not to say that you should tolerate any amount of abuse for the sake of maintaining a relationship. If something bothers you, it's important to discuss it. The problem arises when you criticize instead of addressing specific issues. Specific complaints can be addressed in a mature manner while criticism is a personal attack which immediately puts people in defensive mode. Criticism hardly ever leads to a constructive outcome.

People do change and people should change. But changing the other partner should never be a relationship goal or even a consideration for either of you. Nothing brings about the death of a relationship faster than an ultimatum.

If you're mostly happy with the person she is and you understand that you will naturally grow and change together, it's probably a good time to propose.

You Know You Want to

You should respect the opinions of your friends, relatives, and everyone else you trust, but at the end of the day, you should know why you're proposing and why you want to marry her. It shouldn't be about the next rung of some imaginary ladder, nor should you do it to please her or your family.

You'll be ready to propose when you know you want to do it for yourself and for her, not anyone or anything else.

WHAT TO BE AWARE OF BEFORE TAKING THE PLUNGE

Her Life Goals (And Your Own)

Ideally, your life goals are taking you in the same direction. However, it is okay to not have exactly the same life goals, so long as you've discussed it. Problems usually begin when your goals start pulling you towards different life paths.

It's usually the big goals that have a lasting effect on any relationship. Often, these are related to work, education, housing, or family. If she's working hard on her career or pursuing a degree course that inspires her, that may demand more of her time right now than she has for other things. However, if you agree that you want to spend your lives together, then you should be patient and offer your full support.

By now you should have a good idea of where she sees herself two or three years from now, and if her life goals don't clash with yours, there's nothing to worry about.

Most importantly, be aware of the expectations you're bringing into a marriage and how these will affect the life goals that each of you have. Being in a healthy marriage is demanding for both people. Each will expect the other to fulfill many roles, from confidant to friend, lover, and even therapist. That's bound to be stressful, so you should both find a way to tone down your expectations to a sustainable level.

The romance between you is probably going to fade over time, but that doesn't mean that love has to. Your partner probably can't meet all of your needs, but that's why you have your friends, family, work, and hobbies. You'll both have less time for each other as you become more family oriented, but you can still have quality time together. All these expectations can be brought down to a healthy level without being erased.

The Big Three

In terms of relationships, experts often talk about three big points — money, religion, and children. Finances were discussed earlier in this chapter, so this subject won't get an in-depth discussion in this section. However, finances in the context of a relationship are a bit tricky and some choices and deals will need to be made. Will there be shared finances? Joint accounts or separate? What about savings? All these and other questions need to be answered before the marriage, but they don't necessarily need solid answers before you propose. Just make sure that, on the whole, you're both on the same wavelength.

That leaves religion and kids. These three points are tied to values that remain fairly stable in most people after they've become adults. Therefore, it's a good idea to iron out any kinks before committing to a long-term plan with someone.

A person's religious beliefs are often tied to their identity. If there is a mismatch in matters of the faith, it can cause serious strife. Religion is important to many people and if you can't respect each other's beliefs, the relationship will suffer immensely. The biggest mistake you can make if there are religious differences is to ignore them and hope that they don't come up. They will come up and always at the wrong time, unless, of course, the two of you sit down and talk.

If you're fortunate enough to have the same or overlapping religious views, then it probably won't become a problem. In such case, it's just a matter of discussing some particulars. If you're not that lucky, you will need to start a discussion and try to reach a common ground.

The fastest way to throw a wrench into the wheels of a relationship is to get into a discussion about who's right and who's wrong. It always leads to a disaster of biblical proportions, so to say. Your goal as a couple is to see if you can find a way to overcome them. You may realize that sometimes after discussing religion, the relationship will not hold. Unfortunately, it usually takes couples years of marriage to realize that their religious differences were unbridgeable.

Respecting each other's points of view is a great rule of thumb for any discussion, but it's particularly important with religion. Religion will also make a big impact on the next issue — children.

The first question that should be addressed is whether you want to have children or not. It goes without saying that if one of you wants children and the other doesn't, having children is off the table. This might be a deal breaker. It's not guaranteed that either of you will feel that way forever, but you should acknowledge and accept each other's current opinion on the subject. If you agree to not have children, at least for the time being, which contraceptive methods will you use?

If you do choose to have children, how many and when? Is adoption on the table? Again, many questions will arise and they all need to be addressed in a timely manner.

Decisions about children also tie in to the previous two points. If you do have children, you'll need to decide if they'll be raised religious and, if so, which religion. Children are also a significant expense. Decisions will have to be made about how to finance their futures.

Don't let all this overwhelm you. While these are important issues that need to be worked out, you don't have to decide everything right now. These are the things that you will talk about for months or, in some cases, years. What you need to do is understand one another's point of view so there's something to build from that represents you both.

How She Wants to Handle the Surname

For more traditional couples, this typically isn't an issue. The woman usually takes the man's last name. However, for more progressive couples, it's not quite as clear cut. There's no legal obligation for women to take their husband's last name and many choose not to.

There are also some middle-of-the-road solutions including hyphenated last names and similar options.

It's still somewhat considered the norm for a woman to take a man's last name but that may not be true for long. People identify intimately with their name and if she doesn't want to take your name, it shouldn't be a deal breaker.

If it really matters to you that she takes your name, make sure to communicate that clearly and tell her the reasons why. It might simply come down to traditions that you want to uphold.

For many people who achieve a position of renown in their field, their name becomes their brand. Academics, in particular, become tied to their name and then have to "rebrand" themselves after a name change. In such cases, it's understandable why she wouldn't want to change her name.

Also, you should figure out how to handle the naming of your children. Here too, some people have a much easier time. In some cultures, it is common practice to use both of the parents' original last names. This is becoming common practice in many places and it's a fair way to make sure both names survive. It might not sit well with you, though, which is why it needs to be brought up.

Your relationship most likely won't end over who is going to take whose name. It's just another thing that will eventually come up, so it's better to deal with it sooner rather than later.

In a lot of ways, the content in this chapter is mostly preventative. Rather than wait for problems to arise, it's a good idea to work on them ahead of time. Pay some of the emotional debt in advance, clear up some hard deal breakers, and become closer with the person you want to propose to.

How Committed Are You to Your Respective Careers?

If you want to build a life together, continuing to pursue your respective careers shouldn't necessarily be a problem. There are many couples where both husband and wife are professionally fulfilled. It only becomes an issue if one of you is significantly more devoted to work than the other, and it can lead to feelings of neglect and general anxiety.

For one, it leaves less time to spend together. Spending quality time together is important in every relationship and, for many, a lack of it shows a lack of commitment on the other side. On the other hand, if one is working more and making more money than the other, it's hard to feel like it's an even contribution. Speaking of family, kids can bring further complications to the table.

Children require a lot of time, and if one parent is expected to devote considerably more time to the children it will inevitably make them put their career plans on the back burner.

There's also the practical element of two incomes being better than one. Nowadays, it's especially important to maintain all potential sources of earnings.

This is one of the things that will significantly change over time, so you'll have to make some educated guesses. For example, if one of you is still pursuing an education, that's a big investment that will hopefully pay off later, but it might put some additional financial stress on the relationship. Work evolves and changes and, in an ideal world, you'll be taking on more responsibility and earning more as the time passes. However, that leaves less time to focus on family life. All these things should be discussed, at least briefly.

Careers could also mean moving. If you're closely tied to where you live, expect that moving for work will be hard, especially if it's not something you're comfortable with. Of course, you can't predict everything, but if either of you is on a career path that will likely involve moving, you should talk about it honestly.

The fact is that someone's going to have to provide for the family. It may be one or both of you. The key is to bring up these things early on so they don't become a problem later.

The Time You've Been Together

The average couple spends five years dating before they tie the knot. But you don't have to wait that long if everything feels just right sooner.

That being said, the odds are stacked against whirlwind romances. The truth is that the time you spent together so far isn't enough to determine the strength or the future potential of your relationship. It's only one of many factors to consider.

The longer you've been together the better, but if popping the question after several months feels right, don't let the fact that you've known each other for a short period of time dissuade you from proposing.

Love Can Last, But It Doesn't Stay the Same

Even if you find the absolutely perfect partner, you won't feel infatuated and in love forever. That's nothing to be afraid of because, like all good things, properly nurtured love matures as time goes by. Those first romantic feelings will give way to more mature feelings of love that involve the whole person rather than a few aspects.

Therefore, it's important to avoid the mistake of tying your expectations to those original feelings. Rather, you should base your relationship on the shared values and the ways in which you can work together to create a lasting bond.

The long-lasting, everyday kind of love includes a lot of moments when you don't feel in love at all. What's more, sometimes you'll feel completely disconnected. The key is to see those as single strands in a much larger tapestry that encompasses (hopefully) your entire life. The temptation to sever the ties and run away when things become stale will come up, but don't let fear deny you a chance for a much more rewarding and fulfilling bond.

Fair Fighting

All couples argue and counselors agree that fair fighting is a good way to deal with conflict. It's certainly better than locking the anger up inside. Fair fighting means not using personal attacks or keeping score. If past conflicts don't constantly spark into new ones, chances are you're fighting fairly. And if she fights fairly, that's just more proof that she's right for you.

Keep in mind, however, that the engagement will be a big step for both of you. If there are any tensions between you, smooth them out before the proposal. Take a trip together, do things you enjoy, and just relax. Then, when you propose to her, she won't only say yes, but she will light up like a rainbow.

Any Communication Problems

You don't have to know everything about your partner before you pop the question. However, you do need to be able to bring anything up. Does she understand you even when you are silent? Do you understand her when she sulks? Words matter, but your communication is mostly non-verbal.

That's why it's a lot easier to propose to her when you can communicate your love for her with your whole body. When you propose to her, the way you move, your posture, and your smile will matter. They will be perhaps even more important than the exact words you've rehearsed in front of the mirror.

On the big day, she shouldn't wonder what's in that little box you have conjured up before her like a wizard. She should understand the moment she sees it that you mean love. So, if you haven't told her lately, now is the time to tell her how much you love and appreciate her.

Drugs, Alcohol, and Gambling

Substance abuse problems are very serious in the context of a family, as are runaway gambling habits. However, if it's present before you propose, it should definitely be addressed honestly. A small problem can quickly grow and threaten the very fabric of the relationship if left unchecked.

If you're both young and carefree, it's fine to live your life. But you should also understand that the time will come to dial it down and become more committed to the relationship and your future together. This is often a very touchy subject and it's going to take a lot of introspection if you have any bad habits.

The best thing to do is get it out in the open as soon as possible. The longer it remains under the rug, the harder it will be to deal with it later.

The Type of Ring She Likes

An engagement ring may be a small thing, but it's charged with all the energy and the excitement of the big moment that it symbolizes. Your significant other has all the right to be choosy about it. And if she really likes rings, you need to roll up your sleeves and do your research.

Because diamond grading isn't always exact, you'll need to learn a thing or two about the different types of engagement rings to make the right choice — like the different jewelry styles, the right size, and more. We'll cover this more in depth later in the book. We'll also show you how to figure out her style based on everything from her clothes to her home decor choices.

An engagement ring is a reminder of both the happiness and the responsibilities an engagement brings. And it is, of course, a symbol of the wonderful journey you've embarked on together, to the one who will take you to a truly special destination. Therefore, by the time you propose, you should be ready or at least almost ready, for marriage.

The right ring will make it easier for her to say yes. The engagement ring isn't so much about how much you spend on it. You definitely don't want to skimp on the ring, but you shouldn't go overboard. The real message you send will be the time you invest in learning about it. If you present the ring saying "it's a diamond ring," it won't have the same impact as saying "it's a vintage platinum band with a one-carat yellow diamond in a halo setting." The proposal is a gesture in itself, and details make a big difference.

WILL SHE SAY YES?

If you're not rushing it and the conditions are right for both of you, then you shouldn't have any reason to doubt her answer. But before you propose, consider the signs she may have given you so far. If you've noticed any of these signs, the chances that she will say yes are even higher.

Having said that, don't be afraid of proposing. You will probably be able to intuit quite well whether she wants to marry you or not. Besides, a proposal is not a contract. It's just one more step in the natural progression of a relationship.

- You've discussed marriage

If marriage has been brought up already then the relationship is in the ballpark of being ready. It doesn't need to be an explicit conversation with any carefully laid out plans, but the fact that the topic is being discussed is a good sign. If she seems hesitant in the discussions, it's probably not the right time to propose, but it's still good to talk about it. An open dialogue between you will help you know where you both stand.

- Is she ready in the same ways you are?

There is a long list of things in this chapter that are good signs that you're ready to propose. Most of those can apply to her as well. Has she had a chance to live a full and independent life? Is she over her previous relationships? Is she happy with the person you are or is she hoping that you'll change? Use the same list and think about how it squares with her life. Some of these questions will have to be contextualized but, for the most part, they're good indicators that she's ready for the proposal.

- She talks about your shared future

If she brings up the future often in your conversations, that's a pretty good sign. And if you play a part in the future she speaks of, well, that's more than a sign. It's a pretty strong hint, don't you think? If she doesn't bring up your future together, feel free to be the one that initiates the conversation. A good way to gauge the state of a relationship is by comparing your views on where the relationship will be in a few years.

- She jokes about your engagement

If she jokes about your engagement, she's probably thinking about it. Being lighthearted about it is one way for her to test the ground, and that's another reason for you to act.

- She discusses other people's proposals and weddings

Chances are that someone in your social circle has recently taken the plunge. How did she react? If she was excited about it or told you all the details, just think how much more excited she will be when you propose! Talking about proposals is a very good indication that she's thinking about her own.

But not always. Some people just adore their friends or love weddings. If the other conditions aren't there, her excitement may not indicate much.

- The relationship has been consistent

If there has been a lot of breaking up and making up, it's hard to say whether the relationship has finally stabilized. It's not a good idea to try to use an engagement to fix the issues between you, as it will only put more pressure and expectations on the marriage. If it has been a rocky relationship, be patient. Put in the work to create the right environment of love and trust. Then, when you've put together for a long, stable stretch, you can start thinking about taking your relationship to the next level.

If you've never gotten to a place where you've broken up, it's an excellent sign that you know how to work through problems constructively and that you're probably ready for the next step.

Broaching the Discussion

If your partner hasn't been dropping hints, don't worry. It doesn't mean she isn't thinking about an engagement or that she will hesitate.

Feel free to bring up the engagement when you're ready. Talking about your engagement beforehand is always a good idea. You just need to get the conversation going. There's no need for any conclusions or resolutions right away. Listen not only to what she says, but to how she says it.

You should know her pretty well by now, so you know when it's the best time to bring it up. It could be during a date or over breakfast; ideally it should be a time when you're both relatively stress-free. You could also talk about it without clearly talking about it. Use subtle hints or suggestions to find out where she's leaning first and then segue into the meat of the conversation.

If it makes it easier for you, talk to her friends and family first. They'll probably have some good insights into what she's feeling and where she stands about your relationship. If you trust them, then start there. However, you should only use the information as a way to broach the subject. If what she tells you is different from what you've learned from her family, always take her word over theirs.

You can joke about it if that makes it easier. But when it's time to get serious, get serious. Without pressuring each other, make sure you both know what to expect. If she's not against it, there's no reason for her to say no.

UNDERSTANDING THE TIMELINE BETWEEN ENGAGEMENT AND MARRIAGE

For most couples, engagement is only the last step before marriage. More than making her happy, an engagement will tell her that you're going to marry her before long. An engagement that's neither too long nor too short can help pave the way for the happiness to come.

For most couples, the average engagement length is 12–18 months. It's good to remember that much this time will likely be spent planning your wedding and making sure that everything turns out well. While there is nothing that binds you to marrying within the next 18 months, your fiancée will most likely want to talk about marriage during this time.

An engagement then is not just a prelude to the marriage, but a buildup to it. Both of you should feel comfortable discussing the marriage down to the smallest details a few months after the engagement. Otherwise, you may send her the wrong signals.

After she says yes, take some time to relax and celebrate, but don't delay too much. Planning a wedding is not a simple affair. You'll first need to set a date — deciding whether you want a long or short engagement will dictate what kind of wedding you'll have time to prepare. There's no reason to get into the particulars, but at least decide how long the engagement will last.

Twelve months is a decent timeframe to prepare everything, though weddings have been executed in far less time. The date should respond to how complex you want the wedding to be and how many guests you want to invite. For instance, if you want to marry on a cruise, it's not realistic to expect people to travel halfway across the world on a few months' notice. Also, consider the time of year, as every season presents a different challenge

Take the following timeline as a rough summary of what should happen and when. If you choose to have a shorter engagement, say six months long, most of these milestones can stay pretty much the same. You'll just have to condense them a bit into a shorter time frame. If you go for an extra short engagement of three months or less, you may want to hire a wedding planner. The planner will help keep you on track and take care of most of the finer details for you.

- First, do some optional things, such as engagement photos or create a binder for the wedding planning. Having everything organized will make it easier to check in and gauge how the preparations are going. Some couples opt to have an engagement party, which can be organized as soon as you'd like to. You should also have the guest list 90% done within the first few months.
- It's smart to book the reception venue as soon as possible. Popular wedding venues are in high demand, especially during the summer months.

THE ENGAGEMENT RING GUIDE FOR MEN

- Next up is the bridal party. The guests will have special roles to play and should be given enough time to prepare. If a guest or two can't make it, that's not a disaster. However, if many are missing, it can make things awkward.
- If you hire a wedding planner, you'll save yourself a lot of trouble. However, know that it can be a significant expense. This is the time to start looking for one.
- Booking an officiant is also better done sooner than later. Fill out any associated forms and talk with the person who will officiate the wedding.
- Once the bridal party is set, start choosing vendors. It's better to book well in advance because good caterers and photographers tend to be busy. You'll need the aforementioned photographer, a caterer, a band if you want live music, and a florist. Those are the basics, but every wedding is a unique event, so if you need other services make sure to reserve early.
- Some six to eight months into the engagement, you should order the wedding dress and tuxedo. It can take a while and many adjustments to get everything right, so give yourself and the tailor enough time. You should also start cake tasting around this time.
- At the same time, around six months after the proposal, you should start sending save-the-dates to all the guests. That's a reasonable timeframe to make sure everyone can make the necessary arrangements. If you bought an engagement ring and wedding band together, then you've got one less thing to do. If not, now is the time to purchase wedding bands. It's especially important to get the wedding bands in advance if you want them to have an inscription.
- Invitations are typically sent out 6–8 weeks before the wedding. That's also a good time to start taking care of the final details. For example, a marriage license, if it's needed, should be arranged now. If you choose to write your vows, it's a good time to write them.

ARE YOU READY TO PROPOSE?

- The last month before the wedding is typically when bridal showers are thrown. Bachelor parties are also planned in the last month, typically by the best man.
- In the last few days, the rehearsal dinner usually takes place and any last arrangements are made such as a final headcount, gifts for the bridal party, haircuts, and the like. Double-check that the photographer, caterer, and band will all be ready to avoid any last-minute surprises.
- Finally, the moment you've been preparing for. It's time to get married! Triple check to make sure you have the wedding band.

It bears repeating that this is a very generic timeline that works for a lot of people if they start planning some 12–18 months in advance. A perfectly fine wedding can happen in a much shorter time. It's really about giving all the guests enough time to free their schedule and giving you the time to not have to rush through it.

Hopefully, by now you're a little more confident about knowing whether you're both ready to move on to the next stage. The most important factor is that you *feel* ready to do it.

In the next chapter, you will learn a few things about picking the engagement ring without giving away the secret.

CHAPTER 2
DISCOVERING HER STYLE

SHOULD YOU PICK OUT HER RING WITHOUT HER?

Most men would not have it any other way. A complete surprise, they claim, is part of the experience.

Before you rush to the store, though, you need to consider her preferences. And, of course, you need to know her style. When you know her style, choosing the right engagement ring for her becomes a lot easier. But before we get to that, it's important to understand where you stand on this point.

Here are the main scenarios you may find yourself in:

Point A) She has expressed interest in getting engaged

1. You haven't discussed the engagement ring with her so far. You have some ideas/catchphrases of what she wants
2. You would rather not discuss the engagement ring with her – you want to take her by surprise
3. You want to choose the ring together

Point B) You have never talked about getting engaged before

1. You have not discussed the possibility of an engagement with her. You want to completely surprise her

If you find yourself at Point A, Scenario 3, you can skip this chapter and move on to the next. If you are shopping with her, she'll help guide you towards what she likes. It may, however, be a great idea to read this section anyways. She'll be shocked if you're able to pick a ring that she actually loves, and this chapter will help you do that!

If you find yourself at Point A, Scenarios 1 or 2, or Point B, this chapter is essential for you. Pay close attention to the details. This is a skill that doesn't usually come easy for guys.

Discovering her ring style is not only about making her happy. It's also important for you. When you know her ring style, you can make a better ring choice. More than that, you can increase your confidence and get rid of the anxiety surrounding this crucial part of the proposal. To know what will fit her best, you need know more than just her aesthetic. It's also about who she is as a person, what she likes and dislikes. The ring can even reflect her outlook on life. Style is not only a matter of preference — it reflects our inner nature.

We will try to help you understand her style based on her personality.

One thing you want to avoid is proposing without a ring. An engagement ring may be a small thing, but its symbolism and the role it has come to play in our culture is undeniable. Proposing without a ring could send her the wrong cue. It could tell her, "Hey, I'm only testing the waters here. I'm not really ready to get you a ring yet."

If you don't have the funds to buy an expensive ring, that's absolutely fine, but make sure that you, at least, buy her an affordable ring.

Surprise vs. No Surprise

For some women, an engagement ring can be one of the most beautiful surprises that ever happens to them. It can be one of those special moments they will remember for the rest of their lives, and which they will speak about to their grandchildren many years from now.

- Whether you should pick her ring without her is ultimately a personal choice. Here are the key factors you need to consider before preparing the surprise:
- Whether or not she has expressed her desire to be engaged
- What importance she attributes to style and rings
- Her personality — that is, whether you think she would like to be surprised with an engagement ring
- How well you know her style and taste, which is often influenced by the length of time you've been together

If you still think she would cherish a surprise, it would be a pity for you not to follow through. She will probably consider it a lot more romantic to be taken by surprise.

If you are having any doubts about any of the points mentioned above, it's probably better to play it safe. Some women may prefer to be more involved in the process of buying an engagement ring. For them, trying twenty different rings before finding the right one will be part of the excitement. It can be an adventure in itself, one that they will enjoy deeply. And one that they will remember for a long time.

If your significant other is like that — a shopaholic in the best sense of the word — turning the engagement ring into a big surprise may not be the best idea. That's not to say that she will not love your surprise. She may. But there's no reason for you to deny her the fun of searching together for the right engagement ring, and save yourself from a lot of anxiety in the process.

There's another approach you may want to consider — one which can help you make the right choice but without losing the magic of the surprise. You can take your significant other to a jewelry store (or website) and just window-shop at non-engagement rings and earrings to see which style and cut she prefers.

To summarize: The decision whether to make the engagement ring a surprise or not should depend on her. Knowing all that you do about her — and factoring in the points covered in Chapter 1 — do you think she will like a surprise ring for her engagement? If the answer is a resounding yes (and if she's romantic, and you are romantic, it probably is), then it's time to learn her style.

Are you starting to feel a bit uneasy? Don't worry, you don't need to become a jewelry expert overnight to choose the right ring for her. To make things easier for you, let's navigate the different jewelry styles and what you need to know about each. Learning about jewelry styles is useful not only when you need to buy her an engagement ring, but also next time you want to make her a special present. So, are you ready to make a smart, inspired, and spot-on choice?

UNDERSTANDING THE JEWELRY STYLES

Jewelry today comes in a dazzling variety of styles, and many women like to mix and match these. But don't let that scare you. Learning more about general jewelry styles and vintage styles will provide you with all the useful insight you need. Even if jewelry is a new territory for you, this chapter will guide you step by step through the basics and highlight the important details you should keep in mind.

Precious Metals

Traditionally, jewelers use silver, gold, or platinum as the precious metals of choice. Used since the dawn of time to manufacture jewelry, these metals are the perfect accompaniment to diamonds and other gemstones for creating works of rare beauty and great value. Let's take a more in-depth look at each of these precious metals and how they affect the style of the ring.

- Silver - Durable yet malleable, silver has always been a favorite metal for jewelers around the world. Silver has been cherished throughout history, from the ancient Eastern empires through the great Spanish empire that conquered South America and down to our present day. In the United States, sterling silver is at least 92.5% pure silver.
- Gold - For the ancient Egyptians, gold was the most potent earthly symbol of the sun. For most other nations in the world, gold has been a source of beauty and wealth. Today, some couples reserve

gold for the actual wedding ring, preferring silver or platinum engagement rings instead. Nevertheless, gold remains a favorite choice for engagement rings, whether we are talking about modern styles or museum-grade vintage engagement rings. Because pure gold is too soft for most jewelry, it's often alloyed. In the United States, 14-karat gold is the most common, made up of around 58% gold (compared to 99.9% for 24-karat gold or pure gold). A popular gold alloy for engagement rings is white-gold and rose-gold.

- Platinum - The most expensive of the precious metals, platinum's beauty and rarity made it a favorite in the 20th century when it became a sought-after precious metal for discerning jewelry buyers. And it is not hard to understand why. Stronger than both silver and gold and remarkably durable, platinum is an ideal metal for jewelers who need to create a setting that protects and secures valuable gemstones. Naturally hypoallergenic because of its purity, platinum is an excellent choice if she has sensitive skin.

When looking at engagement ring styles, you shouldn't focus only on the gemstone. Even if the diamond is the centerpiece of the ring, the rest of the ring is important. For example, what if the ring is too small or too large and doesn't fit?

But it's not just a question of practicalities. The craftsmanship and the detail of the ring can enhance the diamond or other gemstone and make the engagement ring truly unique.

GENERAL STYLES

General jewelry styles are contemporary. But you have to remember that just because a woman wears contemporary jewelry, it doesn't mean you can't surprise her with a vintage ring. Before you get to vin-

DISCOVERING HER STYLE

tage styles, however, let's explore first some of the key jewelry styles and figure out which one she prefers.

When trying to determine her jewelry style, it's important not to judge things only by appearances. An expert may be able to distinguish an Art Deco bracelet from a modern one at first glance, but you may not. So, it's a lot safer not to look only at the style of her jewelry. Rather, you want to consider a few other important factors:

- Where she buys her jewelry from
- How much attention she pays to the latest jewelry trends
- What style of clothing she prefers
- Whether she treasures the jewelry pieces she's inherited from her mother or grandmother
- Whether she discusses jewelry a lot with her friends

With these things in mind, let's take a better look at some of the key general jewelry styles you need to know.

Modern

Modern jewelry is, quite simply, the jewelry that is available in most jewelry stores today, whether we are talking about general jewelry stores in malls or boutique shops. Modern jewelry comes in many varieties, but it's usually elegant and sometimes creative. If she follows modern jewelry trends, then that's a pretty good sign she enjoys the freshness and creativity of modern jewelry designs.

Classic

Classic jewelry is usually characterized by its elegance and refinement. Unlike modern jewelry, it is a bit more impartial to trends, leaning more toward timeless designs. These may not catch the eye as readily as modern jewelry, but rather have a more quiet and relaxed beauty. If she enjoys buying jewelry from contemporary jewelers but isn't all that crazy about the latest trends, it's usually a sign that she's more into classic jewelry.

Casual

Jewelry may play a special role during events, but some women wear it effortlessly throughout the day. Casual jewelry is comfortable and elegant and is often intended to complement an outfit rather than to occupy the center stage. It tends to be effortlessly stylish, durable, and versatile. While other styles of jewelry may require certain outfits, casual jewelry — whether we are talking about necklaces, bracelets, or rings — lends itself well to combinations and doesn't necessarily call for a dress.

If she likes to wear jewelry but doesn't make a show of it, casual is probably the style that best reflects her taste. In this case, you may want to avoid an engagement ring that's too ornate or too elaborate, although considering the occasion, you could probably get away with it.

Minimalist

Understated and usually simple, minimalist jewelry often combines modern or classic elements but also adds to them a twist, which is often a creative touch or a new take on a well-known design. Whether we are talking about earrings, necklaces, or engagement rings, minimalist jewelry tends to use simple lines and delicate designs to attract attention.

If she likes minimalist jewelry, you may want to avoid getting her an engagement ring that's big or bulky or that has a very sophisticated setting. She may treasure the proposal itself, but may want a quieter, more delicate engagement ring, such as a simple, single-stone solitaire ring.

Glamorous

Bright and glittering, glamorous jewelry owes a lot to large gemstones, and especially to diamonds. Women who like this style don't want to make compromises, though that doesn't have to mean that they only like big stones. For example, some ring settings, such as the pavé, in which smaller diamonds pave the surface of the ring, could appeal to them just as much as a big solitaire setting with a massive diamond.

A preference for shining and glittering gemstones is a pretty good sign that she likes glamorous jewelry. In other words, you should pay special care to the diamond or the gemstone part of the engagement ring. You shouldn't cut any corners here.

Bohemian

Cool but laid-back, sophisticated but easy-to-wear, the bohemian style can reflect a vivacious but composed personality. Unlike glamorous jewelry, bohemian jewelry doesn't dazzle the eye so readily but is instead more serene. Integrating vintage jewelry with a bohemian style is often quite easy, making this a versatile and engaging style.

If she likes this style, chances are she looks at jewelry made from less conventional materials. She may value the craftsmanship of the engagement ring more than the materials it's made from, though this is not necessarily a rule.

Eccentric

Does she like bold shapes and bright colors and combines them regularly? When it comes to jewelry, an eccentric style is one of the easiest to tell. It catches the eye right away and makes a powerful statement not only about her style but also about her personality. An eccentric jewelry style often combines pieces from all other styles in a chic and charming way.

The eccentric style never gets out of fashion. And the good news is that if she likes this style, you can get away with buying her almost any type of engagement ring, including a very precious vintage ring. Although we've included this style in the 'general styles' section, women who make the eccentric style cool will often not say no to mixing modern and vintage jewelry in unique combinations.

UNDERSTANDING VINTAGE STYLES

When it comes to vintage jewelry styles, it's important to understand the difference between jewelry created today that's made to look vintage and authentic vintage jewelry.

While a skilled jeweler can give a ring a beautiful vintage effect, it won't match the value of an authentic vintage ring. More than their enduring beauty, vintage engagement rings often have a history. And, of course, their value may keep increasing with the passing of time.

Vintage style jewelry can go back to the 19th century, capturing the rich stone arrangements of the Victorian era or the delicate sophistication of Edwardian engagement rings.

When it comes to jewelry, vintage and antique are two terms that are often overlapping, and in this section, we will include antique, Victorian or Edwardian rings in the broader category of vintage engagement rings.

Victorian (1837-1901)

Victorian jewelry captures the quiet beauty and sophistication of an era that's remembered for its romanticism. Unless she's a collector or has inherited some jewelry from her great-grandparents, you can safely assume that she would not own too many Victorian jewelry pieces. This means that choosing a Victorian engagement ring could make your proposal all the more special.

Known for their cluster motifs, which often feature a large gemstone in the center, Victorian engagement rings usually have a gold or silver mounting. If you are looking for a truly special vintage ring for her, you cannot go wrong with a Victorian engagement ring that was been handcrafted over a century ago yet looks just as exciting today.

Just keep in mind, Victorian Rings are very rare. Finding a genuine Victorian Engagement Ring is going to be hard. We only come across four to five Victorian Engagement Rings each year that are good enough for us to showcase in our collection.

Edwardian (1901-1910)

The Edwardian period may not have lasted very long, but its effect on art and culture was undeniable. King Edward the VII, Queen Victoria's son, was one of the most sophisticated monarchs of his day. Edwardian jewelry radiates the sophistication of his court, but it's not necessarily glittering in the way that glamorous jewelry is today. Its beauty is more subdued and delicate, and it takes a real connoisseur to truly appreciate all its nuances.

Known for their eye-catching gemstones as much as for their often-elaborate filigree mounting, Edwardian engagement rings capture the spirit of the fashionable elite that defined the style at the beginning of the 20th century and was to have a profound effect on art. Despite being over 100-years-old, Edwardian engagement rings have an elegance to them that makes them an excellent choice for luxury engagement rings.

Art Deco (1910-1939)

The Art Deco period in architecture and the arts involved quite a lot of experimentation, and that's a recurring theme when looking at jewelry from the period between the First and Second World Wars. Art Deco is sophisticated like few other jewelry styles are, but this sophistication is often contained within its elegance.

Combining craftsmanship with modernist styles, Art Deco engagement rings are some of the most sought-after vintage rings. Delicate yet visually striking, this style shows her that you've gone through some trouble to choose the right engagement ring for her. Art Deco rings stand somewhere in between antique rings from the 19th century and vintage rings from the 1950s and 1980s; they are memorable and, to say the least, very persuasive, which makes it no surprise that they are the most popular vintage style.

Retro (1940s)

Retro jewelry uses old-fashioned designs and motifs to create a charming style that appeals to many women today. However, because the definition of retro jewelry is one that varies greatly depending on who you ask, it's better to look at it in terms of the effect it usually produces rather than just trying to define it along simple lines. This effect is often one of nostalgia

Retro era engagement rings catch the eye with their designs, which are often large or even over-sized. Combining a sophisticated simplicity with old mine diamonds, these rings offer you the opportunity to take her by surprise twice — first with your proposal, and again (but no less exciting) with a unique ring whose compelling beauty will make it so much easier for her to say yes.

Vintage (1950s-1980s)

We've included this as a subsection because when it comes to jewelry, some people also use the term "vintage" to refer to the varied jewelry styles that followed after what is now known as the Retro style. Used in this way, this term defines jewelry crafted in the 50s, 60s, 70s, and up to the 80s. The difference between this type of vintage jewelry and the antique vintage jewelry of the Victorian or Edwardian eras can be quite significant, and it's not just a question of price. The wider availability of gemstones and the economic boom that followed in the wake of the Second World War made large, glittering diamonds a recurring motif for this style of jewelry.

Vintage rings come in many styles. Some use diamonds, other use rubies, aquamarines, or even pearls. While it can be hard to capture the variety of vintage engagement rings in just a few words, they all have that special 'wow' effect that can make her adore you even more, even if she is already head over heels in love with you. And if she happens to have a particular fondness for rings, choosing an engagement ring that was been carefully crafted thirty or forty years ago can only add to the charm and splendor of the special moment you are creating for her.

HOW TO LEARN HER STYLE

You are probably already in love with her style. Not just the way she dresses and the precious little pieces that she summons from her jewelry box and which seem always fit for the occasion, but also all those little details that surprise you about her clothing or jewelry. Now it's only a question of defining her style and understanding it in a way that can inform your ring choice.

Discussing Style with Her

The best way to understand her style is to talk to her about clothes, jewelry, and accessories. You don't want to interrogate her, just get a conversation going. Hearing her talk about why she dresses the way she does and why she chooses specific items can tell you a lot not only about her style, but about her.

Pay attention to the details as they will point you in the right direction. Of course, you have to do some inferring if you want to figure out her style without giving away your intention. If she says, "I don't really like loud jewelry," it could be a sign that she's a minimalist, but then that doesn't exclude the bohemian or eccentric style either, so you really have to consider what she means.

DISCOVERING HER STYLE

As you may have already experienced first-hand, it's easier to figure out her clothing style than her jewelry style. Jewelry is not something that she may wear every day or think about all that often. And even if she likes jewelry a lot, it's a bit harder for the uninitiated (i.e. you) to figure out the many and often subtle differences between apparently similar and yet different types of jewelry. But then that doesn't have to mean that you need to take any chances with her diamond ring. You can figure out her style through her clothes, her existing jewelry, and even the layout of her room. Let's focus on each of these one at a time.

Her Clothes

Does she dress casual or does she like sophisticated clothes? Her clothes reflect her personality, and if you take the time to understand why she dresses the way she does, you'll take much of the guesswork out of choosing the right engagement ring for her.

Even when she rejects trends and conventions, for example, that's a sign that she doesn't like to settle for what she considers "average."

When looking at the clothes she likes to wear, pay attention to the following points, as these are especially important.

- How choosy she is with her clothes?

Consider carefully how much time, effort, and money she invests into her wardrobe. Has she ever saved money to buy a particular dress or pair of shoes? Has she gotten excited when she managed to snatch an otherwise expensive blazer or trench coat at a sale? Then you really need to muster your good taste, or else you could be treading through dangerous waters.

If you cut any corners, if you settle for anything less than the best you can afford, you could make your life a bit harder. Even if she says "yes," she might never forgive you for taking the easy way out with an average engagement ring. If clothes are a big part of her life, you need to buy her a ring that celebrates her taste.

- Does she prefer a casual or sporty style?

If she likes things simple, trying to impress her with a very sophisticated engagement ring may not be the right strategy. In fact, it would be a case of unnecessary bravado on your part and just not the right way to show her how much you love her.

Instead, you could make her love you even more by going for something simple and showing her in this way that you really understand her. Because engagement rings come in so many different styles, you have no excuse not to choose simplicity and elegance over unnecessary glitter. Even if you decide on a vintage ring, going with a simple solitaire arrangement could be a winning strategy.

- How important is comfort to her?

Is she willing to sacrifice her toes and her heels for those red stilettos? Or would she never do such a thing? When it comes to clothes, different women have different threshold levels for comfort, and the excitement over a red pair of shoes or a tight dress may extend this threshold.

But then your significant other may be just the opposite. If she values comfort in clothing and doesn't easily sacrifice it, you definitely want to get her an engagement ring that not only fits her finger perfectly, but that also isn't at odds with the rest of her style. After all, a huge diamond ring could make her uncomfortable if she prefers a relaxed clothing style and is more into sneakers than high-heeled shoes.

A more delicate ring would then be a much more inspired choice.

- Does she have an eclectic or bohemian style?

If she likes to mix and match her clothes and prefers originality over following the latest trends, you may want to stay away from classic ring choices. It's not that she won't treasure a solitaire setting or a big gemstone, but you could be missing an opportunity to truly impress her.

One of the best types of rings you can get her when she has an eye for original clothing is a vintage ring. Fitting both the eclectic and the bohemian styles, a vintage ring can add a special touch to her jewelry collection and make it one of her most cherished possessions. Often times the engagement ring is more memorable than the wedding ring, which is why you really want to make it special.

She's the hands-on type

She works a lot with her hands, gardens, likes sports like tennis or rock climbing. And then on most days, she probably has her hands into something in the kitchen too. If she's like this, you need to get her a ring that's not only pretty, but that will last. It's better then to avoid rings with huge stones or delicate settings that are susceptible to wear and tear. Instead, get her a delicate but robust low-set diamond ring or any other type of ring with a firm and uncompromising setting.

You don't want her to lose the gemstone, do you? If she's a hands-on type and ends up breaking her ring, it's not her fault that you didn't get her something more durable.

But what about vintage rings? Aren't they more fragile than brand new rings? That's hardly the case. In fact, vintage rings are often remarkably resistant — after all, they're still ready to wear 50, 70, or

100 years after they've been crafted.

If you decide to buy her a vintage ring, make sure you choose a ring that's been properly restored and cared for. While a ring may not need as much maintenance as a larger piece of jewelry, it nevertheless needs to be cleaned and checked now and then.

How revealing she is with her clothes

Jewelry needs a bit of skin to attract attention. This is true for bracelets and it is true for necklaces too. If she prefers low-necked shirts and blouses and shorter dresses, and would rather choose short sleeves than long sleeves when given the chance, she is drawing more attention to her jewelry. This may not seem to apply to rings at first, but if she likes to draw attention to her jewelry through what she chooses to wear, you can take that as a cue that she'll love a ring that catches the eye.

But remember that it's not just the glitter that makes the ring. The setting, the precious metal used, the arrangement of the stones, all of this contributes to the 'wow' effect that great engagement rings have. If she likes to dress boldly, a quiet ring is not the best choice for her. Look instead for something that grabs attention.

She likes vintage or retro clothes

Would she rather wear the dresses she's inherited from her mother than shop for new clothes? Maybe her favorite item of jewelry is a brooch she got from her grandmother.

In that case, you may want to avoid a ring that screams 'modern'. Whether she loves everything vintage or is just a bit sentimental about old things, you have a great opportunity on your hands to make her happy with a vintage ring. But don't settle just for any old vintage ring. Try to narrow down the period she is fond of — if she has one — without directly asking her about it. This will make the choice of a ring a lot easier.

Existing Jewelry

Her other jewelry can also help guide your choice. In many cases, it can prove more helpful than her clothing, especially if she changes her clothing style now and then. Her jewelry can offer you clues both obvious and subtle about the best type of engagement ring for her. It can help you choose the right gemstone, the right cut, the right color for the ring, and the right setting, too.

But one thing to note is that you have to be careful about how you go about determining her jewelry style. You don't want to ask her direct questions or get caught searching through her jewelry box. Even asking her what type of jewelry she prefers can give you away. It's far better to take the slow and careful approach, discovering her jewelry bit by bit, without making a show of it.

The first step is to simply pay attention to her jewelry. The pieces she already has can tell you a lot about her style. But also important is how she combines them. Also, it's possible that she has a lot of jewelry but that she wears relatively few pieces, which she keeps rotating.

When looking at her existing jewelry, pay attention to what she actually wears rather than what she has in her jewelry box. Next, let's look at a few more specific pointers.

Predominant Color (Band)

Are most of her bracelets and necklaces yellow gold? Or are they silver? The predominant color of her jewelry is usually the best clue about the right color for the ring part of the engagement ring. Thinking in terms of color here is often more intuitive than thinking in terms of the precious metal itself. That's because if she likes silver or white gold, she probably won't say no to a ring beautifully crafted from platinum. The only hard and fast rule here really is to stick to the predominant color you see in her jewelry.

Things become a bit more complicated if she likes both silver and gold. Which should you choose then? Either of the two would probably be a good choice, but getting the best ring you can afford is still the best approach. That way you know you've done your best. And if the ring is really worth its price, as it should be, it will have a strong effect on her.

And then there's another scenario you need to consider. What if she prefers jewelry from unconventional materials? Base metals like copper, iron, steel, or nickel are staples of many modern jewelry designers. Non-metals may include ceramics, rosewood, ivory, and more. Of course, not all of these are good for engagement rings. Still, if they play a big part in her other jewelry, it's something you should note and try, as much as possible, not to choose a ring that is at odds with them.

You don't need to hire a designer to craft you a unique engagement ring. A beautiful silver, gold, or platinum engagement right will always be an inspired choice. The special occasion that an engagement ring marks ensures that its significance transcends its color and even its style. Still, getting the color right is a great way to make her happy. Gold, for example, is not just yellow or white. There's also rose gold, an alloy of gold and copper, and green gold, an alloy of gold and silver.In the end, the one thing you should do to get the color of the ring band right is pay close attention to her other jewelry and try not to choose a color that is at odds with it. Don't choose a color randomly, but use what you know of her taste in jewelry to make an informed and confident choice.

Diamonds, Pearls, or Gemstones

Precious stones are an essential part of many jewelry pieces. They not only enhance the beauty of the design but add to the value of the piece, often much more than the rest of the materials. The diamond may be the king of the precious stones, and its beauty and value may make it the ideal feature stone for an engagement ring.

Still, you want to look out for any gemstone patterns in her stone collection. Does she show a preference for a particular gemstone? Gemstones include amethyst, aquamarine, pearl, sapphire, emerald, topaz, lapis lazuli, tourmaline, ruby, and many, many others. Even though the same gemstone can come in many different colors — tourmaline, for example, can be anywhere from bubblegum pink to grass green — it can be helpful to group these by their prevalent color for easy reference.

- Red: Ruby or Garnet
- Green: Emerald, Jade, Peridot, or Opal
- Blue: Sapphire, Lapis Lazuli, Aquamarine, Zircon, Turquoise, or Tanzanite
- Yellow: Topaz or Citrine
- Purple: Amethyst
- White: Diamond, Pearl, Moonstone, or Moissanite
- Black: Onyx

If you know that she has a fondness for a particular gemstone, you could consider choosing it as the featured stone of her engagement ring instead of supplemental stone. But since this is a really special occasion, you may want to run that extra mile and get her a diamond. For as Jean de la Bruyere once said, "Next to sound judgment, diamonds and pearls are the rarest things in the world."

There are also some women who will place her birthstone as an accenting stone in their engagement ring. See Chapter 6 to learn more about birthstones and engagement rings.

Room Layout and Style

Her room layout can also offer you important clues about her style. All the care and attention she lavishes on decorating her room says a lot not just about her personality, but also about her style. You can use that insight to make a more informed decision about her engagement ring. Even if she doesn't bother much about the layout and style of her room, that can still say a lot about her style.

Take a moment to consider her room layout and the greater effect it has on the style of her room. Pay attention to the following:

- How sophisticated or simple is her room layout?

Does it contain only practical items that she needs or is it full of furniture and decorations? A simple layout that creates plenty of free space is a pretty good hint that she likes to keep things simple and in order, and so a classic or traditional ring could be just right for her. By contrast, a more sophisticated and innovative layout suggests that she likes things above the fold and will most likely appreciate a ring that's out of the ordinary.

- How much detail is in her room?

DISCOVERING HER STYLE

Empty walls and clear surfaces could mean that she isn't over-concerned with details. But you also have to pay attention to the furniture itself and the other non-decorative items. If the impression you get is that she constantly likes to add detail to her room — whether it's in the form of pictures, statuettes, or other small items — it's a pretty good sign that she will cherish a sophisticated ring. Does she constantly change her room layout?

Compare her room as it was the first time you saw it with what it is today. Has the layout changed a lot? Or does it keep changing every spring? If she likes to reinvent her room all the time — moving things here, then there, and adding and removing furniture — her "fresh" personality may not be all that excited about an engagement ring that looks just like all the other rings she already has.

It's a tough call to make, but it's something to consider.

- What is the interplay between her room layout and her room style?

The layout of the room affects its style, and the style affects the layout. She may have based her room style on a specific layout, so unless she very carefully planned it all right from the start, her room may combine elements from different styles.

This could mean that you should not infer too much about her personality from her room. The style may be more of a product of necessity than an expression of her personality. Key room styles include:

- Modern
- Classic
- New Traditional
- Chic
- Bohemian
- Industrial

- Fun
- Retro
- Vintage
- Rustic / Farmhouse

Placing her room within one of these styles can help you avoid the blunder of choosing a ring that doesn't really reflect her style.

Decoding her Room

Is her room style vintage / rustic / farmhouse-inspired? You may want to avoid a ring that screams modern, though you should consider the style of her clothes and existing jewelry.

Is her room style bohemian, chic, or fun? It's better to avoid choosing a ring that doesn't seem to have a personality of its own, that is, a ring that looks just like all the other rings in the shop window. Proposing to her with such a ring would be the equivalent of showing up for her birthday with an IKEA chair and table set — she will probably thank you politely and then send them off to her mother.

Is her room style retro or industrial? Strike the mark with a ring that's full of retro charm or that has darker hues and a solid metal design that characterizes the industrial style. The industrial style is a bit more vague — for some, it is reminiscent of an old warehouse look, while for others it has more to do with metal surfaces.

Is her room classic or new traditional? If this is also reflected in the clothes she wears and her other jewelry, you want to match the ring style to it. While it doesn't mean you can't buy her a vintage ring or surprise her with an antique ring, you may want to be careful about ring styles that are too loud or that seem to try too hard to impress her, whether it's through the use of unconventional materials or very creative designs. Sometimes, the best way to propose to her is to follow the classic rules and don't try to go over the top with anything, much less with your ring choice.

OTHER WAYS TO LEARN HER STYLE

Her clothes, her existing jewelry, and her room layout should give you a solid understanding of her style. But then there are a few other things that you can do to learn her style, which will in turn guide your ring choice. Pay attention to the following to further increase the probability of her saying "Yes!"

Consider how she dresses for work

If she has to follow a more or less strict dress code for work or wear a uniform, it's important to factor that in. Her work may take up many hours of her week, and during that time she'll have to wear the engagement ring. She may have a different dress style for work, adapted to the requirements of a workplace dress code. Or, in the case of jobs that usually require a uniform, such as flight attendant, schoolteacher, or company representative, where she may not have much of a choice in terms of her outfit style, she may still use accessories or jewelry to add a few personal touches to her look.

Just consider for a moment the flight attendant's scarf and the many different ways in which an air hostess can wear one — from the close, warm, and quiet neck wrap with a fancy braid, to the flowing shoulder duster and loop tie.

For many women, style is often strongly defined by the clothes they wear at work, so her work outfit is something you should really pay attention to. Is it all about style and elegance, or does comfort play a big part in it? Often she may aim for a balance between the two. Define her work outfit style in simple terms such as casual / formal, relaxed / sober, simple / sophisticated, comfortable / elegant, and consider how the type of ring you buy her (more about ring types later in this book) goes with that.

Pay attention to the music she likes

Would she rather strum a guitar than go to the opera? Is she more into folk and blues than the more upbeat rhythms of contemporary music? By now you probably know what music she listens to. Use that to better understand her personality. It will help you not just to choose with her the soundtrack for the wedding, but could prove useful in the short term by making your choice of a ring a little easier.

Pay attention to what she wears on weekends

During the week, her job may limit her style. Even if her job doesn't come with a strict dress code, she may still make compromises to achieve that level of comfort that she needs to get through the day without feeling like her sweaty clothes and heavy jewelry are dragging her down to an early retirement. But on weekends, there's nothing to hold her back, and don't be surprised if her style blooms and undergoes a massive transformation.

Register the changes — whether there's a significant increase in the amount of jewelry she wears, whether her clothes become all of a sudden more sophisticated, whether the pants and sweaters get replaced by long and flowing dresses. If this is the case, you'll have to take her duality for what it is. Your engagement ring shouldn't be just for the weekend version of her but must be adapted to her workdays too.

If you live together, pay attention to what she's wearing at home. If it's all slacks and sweatshirts, comfort is probably important for her. It doesn't mean she doesn't care to elaborate on her style, only that you don't want to go all glittery with your choice just for the sake of making a great impression. An engagement ring is, after all, a practical thing that she will likely wear daily for at least a few months before she trades it for a wedding band. More than aesthetic beauty, it has to be suited to all the transformations in style she may undergo, all the while staying pretty comfortable too.

Be extra mindful to what accessories she wears during special events

Her friend's wedding, her sister's birthday party at the posh restaurant, her promotion party, her nephew's graduation — any such events can tell you a lot about her style. If you notice any patterns — she prefers one kind of jewelry color over all the others, she never wears particular gemstones — use it to guide your ring choice. It's often during these occasions that she has a chance to make the most of her full range of jewelry. If you're lucky enough to have one of these events scheduled up, note what she wears and how she does it.

Be aware of her love of the outdoors

Where you live and what you do in your free time can also tell you a lot about her style. If she's an outdoor person, she may toss away the bracelets and rings and change her business suit for a hiking suit or pair of overalls without second thoughts. We've already touched on whether she's a hands-on person or not, but there are cases when she's not but still spends a lot of her time outside running, cycling, hiking, trekking.

Outdoor activities could mean she has to do away with most of her jewelry, abandon all style to functional and comfortable clothing, and put on gloves. The engagement ring you give her should be the one piece of jewelry that survives this transformation. Her love of the outdoors doesn't have to narrow down your ring choice too much, though. It should only give you yet another reason to choose something that's durable and doesn't get in the way of her doing the things that she wants to do.

What questions to ask her friends and family

Asking her friends and family to help you define her style is yet another helpful way to get the ring right. But you have to go about this carefully. That is, you have to go to the right people. Her best friend may know more about her style than you can ever know, but if she's a gossip and can't stop herself from ruining the surprise, she may give your surprise away. Same with her mother or sister.

If you do choose to ask, don't do it prematurely. Wait until you've done all the beginning research and then ask shortly before buying the ring and proposing to her. Not only will you already see the bigger picture, but it will also give less time for the gossip to slip back to her.

Now, let's look at some of the key questions you want to ask.

1. What jewelry style does she prefer?

Don't be surprised if different people see her style differently. You're not searching for a consensus here, but for the common thread you can follow to make the best possible decision. It's better to focus

DISCOVERING HER STYLE

on the jewelry style rather than the broader clothing style. It will likely provide you with more details that you can act on when the time comes to choose her ring.

2. Has she even mentioned a type of engagement ring that she would like?

Don't be surprised if she has. She can discuss an engagement ring much more easily with her girlfriends or sisters. She may have even already chosen out her dream ring.

3. Do you think she would like a diamond engagement ring?

You want to make absolutely sure that a diamond would be the right precious stone for her ring. Most of the time it is the safest option, but hearing it from someone who knows her will give you that extra bit of confidence when you go to buy her ring. It's hard to find a woman who doesn't like diamonds. But some women may have a fondness for a particular gemstone that goes back to their childhoods or a particular belief they have, and that's something you shouldn't ignore.

4. Would a vintage diamond ring suit her?

Most women won't need any description of what a vintage ring is — they just know. But if you sense any hesitation, you may want to use the knowledge you've accumulated so far from this book and explain to them exactly what a vintage ring is. Don't be afraid to be specific, they will understand.

If she is very concerned about the environment or if she is sentimental by nature, she may only want to buy a vintage ring.

5. What ring style do you think would **not** suit her?

Ask them what rings will suit her and you will probably get as many different answers as the number of people you ask, because their answers will likely be a reflection of their own taste. Remember: it's you who has to fit all the pieces of the puzzle together and make the final decision, because by now, you should know her better than anyone else in the world. You should go to her friends and family for guidance, not for the definitive answer.

Asking them what she doesn't like will usually give you a lot more clear direction and consensus than asking for what she does like.

Who Else to Ask

It's not just her friends and family who can be helpful at this stage. Her colleagues from work could prove very useful as well — especially if one of them got engaged recently and showed your better half her ring, which in turn made her say something like "Oh, what a beautiful ring! I want one just like that!"

Female neighbors could also guide your choice, especially if she's spending time at their houses, going with them to the gym, or taking part in other community activities.

Sometimes, a neighbor who has recently gotten engaged may turn out to know a lot more about your partner's style and the right ring choice she would make than just about anyone else in the world.

Also, if there's anyone in your social circle with a solid experience in engagements and weddings, you may want to ask them too, regardless of their sex, and even if they don't fall into either the friend or the neighbor category.

Last but not least, a reputable seller of engagement rings should

DISCOVERING HER STYLE

also be able to help you find the right ring for her. By telling them a bit about your better half's style, you make it easier for them to guide you in the right direction. You could call them in advance or schedule an appointment.

In the end, don't forget that while it's usually better to talk to others face to face about something as important as your better half's ring style, you can also use email, phone, and social media to reach people that otherwise wouldn't be accessible, such as colleagues from work or her expat sister from, say, New Zealand.

Which Websites to Look At

The web, and social media in particular, can be another rich source of information. You should start with her own social media accounts, which can serve as a record of her style much better than your own memory of what she wore last week at that party you both went to — can you remember the color of her shoes, let alone the bracelets and earrings she wore?

We at Estate Diamond Jewelry have hundreds of thousands of social media fans and they're constantly sharing our pictures to their profiles. Many of our customers are boyfriends who found their girlfriend's "dream ring" by scrolling through their social media accounts.

Look at her profiles as a visitor would, and if you're not the squeamish type, don't be afraid to go back to her online style records before the time you've got together. If scrolling through a few pictures of her and some of her Exes is the price you have to pay for gleaning that extra bit of information that can help you make the absolute best ring choice.

Once you're done with the networks she's active on — and you should be able to figure these out without too much trouble — turn your attention to the most visual social media sites on the web. These sites set many of today's fashion trends, and they are packed not just with examples of styles, but with influencers full of advice for people in your shoes.

Take your time to check these key sites. Use the search box to type "engagement ring styles" and other related keywords and enjoy the visual treat. Note that if you don't have an account on these sites already, you will have to create one for free to be able to access all the content.

Here is a list of the four most important social media accounts to search her profile for posted rings:

- Pinterest | www.pinterest.com

Pinterest users are constantly uploading images and videos and creating many pinboards related to fashion, jewelry, and engagement rings.

I'd like to single out Pinterest because if she has an active Pinterest account, there is a very strong chance that she has already pinned a bunch of engagement rings on one of the boards.

- Tumblr | www.tumblr.com

This is the preferred visual blogging platform for many fashion bloggers. The rich blend of visual content and text makes Tumblr a valuable source of information related to engagements and weddings.

- Instagram | www.instagram.com

Instagram can tell you a lot about the latest fashion and engagement ring trends too. For many women, it's become the go-to site for photos snapped with their mobile cameras, much more so than Facebook. However, on Instagram it's mostly about the images — don't expect to get as much textual info as on other networks, excluded of course other users' comments. If you see a picture of an engagement ring, you may have to go digging to work out where it is from.

- Facebook | www.facebook.com

Facebook can help you discover the reactions she may have had when friends or family members got engaged or married. What's more, the Facebook content timeline allows you to find events she attended and jump straight to them without having to browse through too much content. Facebook can help you discover her reactions to her friends' or family's engagement ring photos and determine what she likes and what she doesn't.

HOW TO FIND HER FINGER SIZE

And now we have come upon one of the most challenging aspects of the whole engagement — getting her ring size right.

If you could ask her, it would be easy, but if you want to keep it a surprise, asking her may ruin it. Resist the temptation to ask any indirect questions about her ring size or you've come all this way only to give yourself away. Instead, choose one of the following tried and tested methods to wisely to secretly figure out her finger size.

"Borrow" her ring (when she takes it off)

This should be a ring she's currently wearing or one that she has worn until recently. Better to avoid older rings as finger sizes may increase or decrease with time. But whatever you do, don't ask her to just pass you on the ring. "Borrow" it when she isn't paying attention

— while she's showering, out in the garden pruning the roses, on the tennis court, or whenever she takes it off.

Have a slip of paper and a pencil ready, and when the opportunity arises, put the ring on the paper and trace it, first the inside of the ring, and then the outside. This is the simplest and most accurate method to get her ring size right. Alternatively, you can also have a look at her jewelry box, but make sure she's not around. You will also have to make sure that it's a ring that she wears on her ring fingers or pointer fingers. The other fingers will have different sizes.

Hold her hand and compare

If she never takes her ring off or doesn't wear a ring all the time (yet), don't worry. There's another way to figure out her ring size. It's not as accurate, and you have to be discreet about it so that you don't give yourself away. But it should give you a pretty good idea about her ring size. Next time you hold hands, look to see whether any of your fingers is a similar size to her ring finger.

Even if it's only the upper part of your finger, it can help you to test out potential rings for her. One thing you should know is that when fingers are cold they become smaller than at warm temperatures, so it's better to avoid this method when you are walking with her outside gloveless in late fall or winter.

However, this technique is far from perfect and may require you to resize the ring after the proposal.

Ask her friend or sister

Her sister or best friend may already know her ring size. For example, they may have tried rings together ("Oh, what a nice ring!" "Want to try it? Here."). If you've not been able to measure her ring size accurately already, her friend's or sister's guidance can rescue you. It's also good to ask them if you're just not sure about the size despite your measurements.

Her friend's hands should be much more like hers than yours (most of the time at least) and that will prove very useful. Often, the best person to ask is the one who got engaged or married recently, as it's very likely that she and your better half have discussed rings already.

A good fit means her ring is neither tight nor loose, and she won't have to worry about losing it or not being able to take it off later to put on a wedding band. As a starting point, you should know that the average ring size for the average-sized woman in the US (5 feet 4 inches tall) is between size 5 and size 7. More about ring sizes later.

Find Out If She Believes in Spending a Lot on the Engagement Ring

She may be excited about the idea of getting engaged one day, and she may look forward to the proposal and the engagement ring itself, but maybe she values other things more than jewelry and wouldn't want you to go out of your way to buy her the most expensive engagement ring you can afford. Instead, she'd rather have you settle for something original and authentic.

Overspending on her engagement ring can be as bad as settling for something cheap. If the value of the ring is not an important consideration for her, you need to focus on the style of the ring more than its actual value. This section is not about your budget or how to save money on the ring (we'll cover that more in depth in Chapter 4). Rather, it's about making sure that you're getting the style right.

It's perfectly fine to have the budget for a luxury engagement ring but settle for something more fitting that ultimately won't cost all that much. At the same time, you need to consider how important the actual value of the engagement ring is for her. If, so far, she or any of her friends have dropped any hint about the value of the engagement ring, take it. If she said she'd rather go to Hawaii or Australia than be spoiled with a super-expensive ring, act on that bit of advice.

But if she is at the other end of the spectrum and cherishes the idea of a diamond engagement ring, you don't want to disappoint her. Get her the best you can afford.

Apart from what she actually says — again, it's best not to ask her directly — also consider any comments or advice her friends or family let slip. Pay attention to any comments she may leave on social media related to engagement rings. If some celebrity or another spent $250,000 on an engagement ring and her reaction was something like "I'd settle for a $25,000 ring and use the rest to start an AI-programming business," then she's making things easy for you, don't you think?

CHAPTER 3
A GUIDE TO ENGAGEMENT RINGS

A wedding ring is very different from an engagement ring. Wedding rings serve the mostly mechanical function of publicizing a person's marital status. Engagement rings, on the other hand, are a symbol of choosing a person to be your partner in life. The diamond engagement ring is more than just an outward symbol — it represents an internal facet to the relationship and often ends up getting passed down through generations.

You'll might be under some pressure to choose the right engagement ring. There are so many choices. It can really seem overwhelming to an inexperienced buyer. You might think that — given all of those choices — the perfect ring has got to be out there somewhere, but don't drive yourself crazy. The right engagement ring is the one that you think best summarizes what she means to you. Once you understand a few basic criteria about rings and jewels, it will be easy to find your ring.

The first and primary factor that will go into your decision is the diamond you want to use. Modern diamonds are cut very precisely and tend to be crafted into the shape that provides the best appearance. Diamonds are graded on several criteria of quality by certified laboratories. You'll be spending a very significant part of your budget on the diamond alone, so it will pay off to learn about them.

Getting the right diamond quality and matching it up with the right setting is a bit of a balancing act. It will take some effort to even establish what kind of ring you'd like to buy, but this book will give you all the knowledge you need to make an educated decision.

The other part will be the ring. Several precious metals are used for the creation of engagement rings and that will be important to know as well. On top of the different metals, the style of the ring will make a big difference on the diamond you will choose. There will be something like a feedback loop with the ring and the diamond on either side. Your goal is to strike the perfect balance to accentuate the stone as much as possible without breaking the bank.

BRIEF HISTORY OF ENGAGEMENT RINGS

It's hard to pinpoint the exact origin of engagement rings, but there are many references to rings in betrothal ceremonies throughout history. One of the very first written accounts of a marriage being marked by gifting jewelry is in the Hebrew Bible. When Abraham sets about finding a wife for Isaac, he sends his servant Eliezer to find a kind and generous woman. The woman Eliezer ends up finding is Rebecca, and he gives her a golden nose ring and bracelets to seal the pact.

There's some evidence that ancient Romans used engagement rings as well. In fact, some records show that Romans gifted two rings — an iron ring to be worn in daily life, and a gold ring to be worn in public. The earliest explicit reference to engagement rings can be found in the Visigothic Code from the 7th century. In this code, the ring is described as a pledge, and even though nothing is committed in writing, the pledge could not be reversed under any circumstances.

It wasn't until the mid-1400s that the diamond ring entered the historical stage. Archduke Maximilian of Austria reportedly commissioned a diamond engagement ring to mark his betrothal to Mary of Burgundy. This started the tradition of using diamonds in engagement rings that we still observe today. Engagement rings rose in popularity slowly until the Victorian Era, when they became much more trendy.

Since that first recorded diamond engagement ring, many changes to the style and tradition have taken place. Queen Victoria's reign was influential in many ways and jewelry design is certainly one of them. Victorian-style rings are still very much in vogue today. In the early 1900s, there was a rise in the use of platinum as the metal of choice for engagement rings, and more details and intricacies were added to the design.

Today, only the woman typically receives an engagement ring, but that convention has been slowly changing. Many couples choose to use two engagement rings, one for the man and one for the woman. The engagement rings worn by men have been dubbed "management rings."

Around 1870, enormous diamond deposits were discovered in Africa and this set a whole new course for jewelry in general but engagement rings in particular. Given the newfound abundance of diamonds, their scarcity would no longer justify their price, so interested parties set out to increase their demand exponentially. After World War I, the demand for diamonds was at an all-time low, which sparked concerted efforts to place diamonds as a symbol of courtship and the union of marriage.

The idea of diamonds in engagement rings is traced back to ad campaigns in the 1940s that were aimed at reviving interest in diamonds. The N.W. Ayer ad agency created a very comprehensive advertising plan that involved movie stars and lectures at schools to bring diamonds into the forefront of public consciousness. The popular phrase "diamonds are forever" was created as part of that advertising. Clearly the idea took hold, because today we take it for granted that diamonds are the stone of choice for engagement rings.

Diamonds were used in engagement rings before then, but the idea took hold in earnest following the advertising efforts. Even the British royal family is said to have helped by wearing diamonds in favor of any other gems.

Whatever the origins may be, engagement rings have been an important part of our culture. Buying an engagement ring is more than just spending money on jewelry. There is a lot of historical baggage associated with it, and it's a good way to not only show your love but also maintain a link to our collective past.

HOW MUCH SHOULD YOU SPEND?

There is no shortage of advice about the correct amount to spend on an engagement ring. This advice often tends to be outdated or just plain outlandish. The traditional rule of thumb has been to look for something in the two-month salary range, meaning you'd spend about as much as you make in two months. For many people, this can be unrealistic and doesn't take into account their financial situation. For some, it may be unbelievable irresponsible.

The engagement ring is not supposed to be a massive financial burden. If the price hurts too much, you're spending too much!

The ring that you buy doesn't need to be a complete surprise. Even if you want to make your engagement unexpected, you should have an idea of what your girlfriend wants. A simple guiding principle is to never go into debt for an engagement ring. The responsible choice for you may be to spend $10,000 or it may be to only spend $100. That's why it's very important to create a budget from the outset and stick to it.

For a much better idea of what to spend, one that takes into account your financial goals, you can use our engagement ring price calculator (www.estatediamondjewelry.com/engagement-ring-calculator). The calculator will take many more factors into account than just your salary. Things like your debt and lifestyle play a big role in how much you should be willing to spend. Of course, even the calculators won't tell you the whole story. Any system that claims to be all-encompassing probably wasn't made with your best interest in mind.

There are many things that go into choosing the right ring that we will explain in this chapter, but for now, you want to think about two major concepts with regards to the price: your partner's expectations and your financial circumstances. With that in mind, consider your income and projected expenses in the coming months.

Other significant expenses will come into play even if you're not ready at the moment. The best-case scenario is that you've had your proposal in mind for a long time. That way, you can rely on the savings you've set aside for a ring. Finally, if you're expecting growth in your job, it will give you a little more leeway in deciding your budget.

Another good way to approach the issue is to use a national average as your guide. The average price paid in the US for an engagement ring has been dropping in recent years. Depending on the source, ring prices for 2019 are estimated to be around $6,800. This is probably the simplest way to choose your spending limit. If you want to be a little more specific, you can choose a number closer to the top or bottom of the distribution.

The biggest contribution to the ring's cost is usually the diamond. You can take the diamond as a starting point when determining the price. The average diamond in the US is 1.10 carats, so you can start with a suitable diamond and choose the band accordingly. The problem with this method is that all diamonds are not created equal. The same 1.10-carat diamond can vary in price by up to tens of thousands of dollars. If you choose to take the carat size into consideration, be sure to continue reading so you learn about the other criteria that diamonds are graded by.

You're probably in a committed and mature relationship if marriage is the next step. In this kind of a healthy relationship, you shouldn't feel like you need to make this decision alone. Have an honest conversation with your girlfriend about her expectations and your shared financial goals. Remember that you'll eventually be combining your finances to some degree, so you should take into account not only your circumstances but hers as well. By having this conversation, you can agree on a price bracket but also get an idea of where her tastes lie in terms of the style of ring.

The amount you spend on the ring will inevitably be compared to your other expenses. If she perceives that you're willing to spend heavily on other areas in your life but are frugal about the ring, that could create some friction.

Ultimately, the ring you want to buy should be meaningful. That won't always be tied to price; it could be a ring that resembles a family heirloom, or it could mean buying a new gem for an old band. In any case, keep in mind that you're expressing your love and devotion with this ring, not making a statement about your income.

UNDERSTANDING THE 4 C'S OF A DIAMOND

Now that you have an idea of how much money you want to spend on the ring, you need to learn how to pick out the right one. The best way to start your journey is by learning how diamonds are graded and how their grade affects their price.

Diamonds around the world are graded using the so-called 4 C's. This grading system was created by the Gemological Institute of

America (GIA). The 4 C's helped to make a lot of progress in establishing trust and dispelling confusion about gems and their value. To an outside observer, the price of diamonds may seem a little arbitrary, but the 4 C's are only the first step in a broader grading system that provides the information to establish a diamond's quality.

The 4 C's stand for a diamond's clarity, cut, carat weight, and color. Each of these aspects is evaluated for quality and graded on a scale. The following is a short overview of each of the C's to explain exactly what it is that's being graded.

A quick Note on Lab-Grown Diamonds

There is a separate class of diamond that has entered the market in earnest somewhat recently — the lab-grown diamond. The technology to create synthetic diamonds has existed since the early 20th century. Diamonds that were produced then were of poor quality and easily inferior to natural diamonds. Since those early days, the process has been improved to the point that lab-grown diamonds now have a high degree of brightness and clarity.

This type of diamond has sparked a lot of contention, and it's no wonder. The quality of lab-grown diamonds can be controlled to a minute detail. Even impurities and inclusions can be added as necessary to simulate the natural process. However, for many people in the industry this presents a departure from the spirit of diamonds.

The feeling is mirrored by consumers as well. A minority of people (fewer than 20% according to research by the Diamond Producers Association) see lab-grown diamonds as being authentic. It's true that they are chemically equivalent, but they lack an intangible quality that natural diamonds have. Natural diamonds are imperfect in very unique ways related to their formation, and it is precisely these imperfections and the extreme environment that produced them that hold special appeal.

Lab-grown diamonds are graded using the 4 C's, but the process is a little different. Once they are determined to be synthetic, they undergo grading under slightly modified criteria. Cut grading is exactly the same but the remaining scales are modified to better suit the nature of man-made stones. The grading report will explicitly state that they are laboratory-made.

While the 4 C's are important to gem experts in determining quality, their value to you lies in how they can help you choose the right diamond without overpaying. Seeing diamonds in person with an experienced jeweler will help you figure out which of these are important to you.

Our personal opinion is to steer far away from lab-grown diamonds. Their price is somewhere in ballpark of 30% less but they are (currently) almost impossible to resell. Buying a lab-grown diamond is a very risky choice.

Diamond Clarity

Clarity is the lack of inclusions and blemishes in a diamond. Diamonds are a very unique form of crystal mostly composed of carbon. When they are being formed, the environmental conditions around them can cause minute imperfections to appear. These imperfections are divided into two types depending on where they occur within the diamond:

- Inclusions are small flaws that occur within a diamond while it's being formed. The position of inclusions relative to the stone is very important. Inclusions intrude on the light as it passes through the diamond, removing some of the brilliance. They are essentially the result of irregular crystal growth.

- Blemishes are the other type of imperfection, but these are visible on the surface of the stone. Sometimes blemishes are the result of inclusions that have ended up on the surface, but they are more commonly man-made. Natural blemishes are often removed by polishing, so if any blemishes exist, they are most often the result of the cutting process.

A diamond's clarity is an evaluation of the size, amount, and visibility of these flaws and how they affect the stone's appearance. The closer a diamond is to being perfectly clear, the more valuable it is. The clarity scale was developed to remove any ambiguity in the process of determining clarity.

Clarity is measured on a scale from Flawless (FL) to Inclusions 3 (I3). Flawless diamonds are the rarest, and they appear to have no blemishes or inclusions at 10x magnification. Diamonds graded I^3 have inclusions that are visible to the naked eye. Graders also check if the diamond has been treated to improve clarity.

When choosing a diamond, you should look for one that isn't visibly included or blemished. This will most likely be a diamond that is Very Slightly included (VS1 or VS2). It may be the case a diamond you find has lower clarity but still fits well with your ring. Here is the entire scale from the GIA for reference:

- Flawless (FL) - No inclusions or blemishes are visible to a skilled grader using 10x magnification.
- Internally Flawless (IF) - No inclusions and only blemishes are visible to a skilled grader using 10x magnification.
- Very, Very Slightly Included (VVS1 and VVS2) - Inclusions are difficult for a skilled grader to see under 10x magnification.
- Very Slightly Included (VS1 and VS2) - Inclusions are minor and range from difficult to somewhat easy for a skilled grader to see

under 10x magnification.
- Slightly Included (SI1 and SI2) - Inclusions are noticeable to a skilled grader under 10x magnification.
- Included (I1, I2, and I3) - Inclusions are obvious under 10× magnification and may affect transparency and brilliance.

Becoming intimately familiar with the clarity scale isn't as important to you as looking for a diamond that is "eye clean." Eye clean diamonds are those that appear free of flaws to the naked eye when viewed from a short distance. This is a very basic guideline and will depend on a variety of factors such as gem size and lighting conditions.

If you inspect a diamond carefully and can't find any dullness or imperfections, there's no reason to spend more on a higher grade. On the other hand, if your goal is to make a statement that will be passed down in your family, a much higher-quality stone is preferred. Typically, a diamond rated SI1 or VS2 is as low as you can go without seeing any obvious drop in quality, but every diamond will be different.

Diamond Cut

When light hits a diamond, it's broken up and reflected rather than passed directly through it. A diamond's cut is a measure of its symmetry and polish, which directly impacts the diamond's interaction with light. A precise cut with the right proportions will deliver the best fire, brightness, and scintillation.

Brightness refers to the white light that is reflected internally and externally to the diamond. Fire is the degree to which the diamond breaks up the light into colors attractively. Scintillation is, simply put, the sparkle that a diamond produces. Further in this chapter you'll learn about those terms and how to use them. These three factors are largely determined by the quality of the cut.

From best to worst, the grades of a cut are:

- Excellent
- Very Good
- Good
- Fair
- Poor

There are many things to take into consideration when creating an attractive stone, and cut often comes into conflict with a diamond's weight. A well-cut diamond commands a higher price, but people often prize weight over cut quality. This puts the cutter in a position of balancing the best possible cut while sacrificing the least amount of stone.

In the past, a rough diamond could potentially yield a much better cut, but cutters were hesitant to reduce the weight. Nowadays, diamonds are scanned by computers. Computer planning allows for the plotting of all the inclusions and mapping of the best saw-able planes to minimize waste.

The cut is extremely important when selecting a diamond and it's the most technically challenging aspect to determine. The broad number of variables that affect the quality of a cut makes it a good stand-in for a diamond's attractiveness.

Now, you might be wondering how to use a stone's cut grade when choosing a diamond.

The basic rule of thumb is to spend the most on the cut. If any single factor can be said to influence a diamond's appearance the most, it's the cut. This is why cut grades will impact the price so significantly. It's a good idea to buy the diamond with the best cut you can afford over a larger or clearer diamond with a worse cut.

If you're selecting a round diamond, the cut will matter more. Look for round diamonds with an Excellent or Very Good cut grade. You can get away with lower-quality cuts in other shapes.

The grading for a vintage or antique cut stone will be very different than that of their modern counterparts. Stones that were cut prior to modern cutting techniques (roughly before 1950) will rarely be graded higher than Good or Very Good.

Diamond Carat Weight

Carat weight is probably the characteristic that gets the most attention in popular culture. A carat is a unit of mass and it stands to reason that the more diamond you have, the more it is worth — but this isn't always the case. One metric carat is defined as 200 milligrams. But don't confuse a diamond's carat weight with the karat rating of gold, which measures purity. One uses a "c" and the other uses a "k" for a reason.

Carats are divided into 100 "points" which allow for much more accurate measurements. Therefore, a 0.25-carat diamond will weigh 50 milligrams and so on. As carat weight increases, the value will typically increase as well. On equal terms that will hold up, the other 3 C's will have a huge impact on value as well. For example, a smaller stone could easily be worth more than a larger one if it's of a higher quality.

There will be a meaningful difference between how large a diamond actually is and how large it appears to be. As with the other characteristics, this one will be affected by the setting, size of the person's finger, and many other factors. For instance, an emerald cut produces a much larger table (the top facet of a stone). Emerald-cut diamonds look much larger than other diamonds of the same weight.

Because a diamond's price rises so steeply as a consequence of carat weight, you should examine a diamond in its setting rather than rely solely on the carat. You could find a stone that appears larger than another stone of the same size that is shaped differently.

Another thing that's important to consider is that carats aren't valued uniformly. Larger stones are much rarer so two 1-carat stones will be valued less than a 2-carat stone, and so on. You can think of this as reverse wholesale, where the larger a diamond is, the more you're paying per unit instead of paying less for bulk.

Another consideration is that some weights are "magic sizes." Half-carat, three-quarter-carat, and one-carat are seen as breakpoints in diamond size and they result in an outsized increase in price. The reason for this is somewhat arbitrary — round numbers just sit better with people. Owning a 0.95-carat diamond ring doesn't have the same weight to it as owning a 1-carat diamond ring, even if these tiny variations in size are imperceptible to the untrained eye.

Diamond Color

A diamond's color actually refers to its lack of color. Pure diamonds are colorless and much more valuable than tinted ones. It's important to note that not all colors are undesirable — red diamonds, for instance, are the most expensive kind of diamond. These special diamonds are rated on a different scale.

Color is evaluated on a scale from D (colorless) to Z (light yellow or brown), skipping A, B, and C to avoid confusion with other scales. The closer a diamond is to a "D" rating, the purer it is. The differences from one color grade to the next are often not perceivable to the untrained eye. Therefore, they tend to be less important when choosing a diamond. However, the color can have a very significant impact on the price of the stone.

Determining a diamond's color requires laboratory conditions where it is compared to a master set of diamonds representing the scale. Generally speaking, you should review each diamond you're considering rather than rely on the color grade. If the tinting of a diamond doesn't impact its brilliance and sparkle under normal conditions, it is probably clear enough. In most cases, diamonds rated from D to J will appear colorless.

Another important aspect of choosing color is the setting. A completely pure diamond in a vintage gold setting might not have the colorless quality you're trying for. In some cases, a diamond with a slight tint may be better suited to emphasize the lack of hue.

Most naturally occurring diamonds fall within the range of the D-Z scale. However, different hues do happen under the right conditions. These colored diamonds are referred to as fancy-color diamonds. They are much rarer and consequently tend to be more expensive than pure white diamonds.

The main criterion for evaluating colored diamonds is the intensity of the color. They possess other visual characteristics of diamonds, but those are considered less important than the color in this case. Broadly speaking, fancy-color diamonds with a rich and deep shade are graded higher than those with slightly pale shades of color.

The color in these diamonds is rated on its hue, saturation, and tone. The diamond's hue is the characteristic color it displays, be it pink, brown, or yellow. Saturation refers to the strength of the color, and tone measures how light or dark the color appears. The hue is matched to 27 recognized hues in fancy-color diamonds and its relative intensity is measured by a "Fancy Grade." So, a pink diamond with a strong hue and saturation might end up being graded "Fancy Intense Pink."

In addition to the 4 C's, colored diamonds receive a special grading report which reviews the quality of their color and the source. Sometimes diamonds are treated to achieve a different color and that treatment will be accounted for in the report. Only natural diamonds are graded for their color.

OTHER DIAMOND FACTORS

The 4 C's we just covered correspond to a grading method developed as an objective way to rate diamonds. However, they're far from the only considerations for an attractive stone. Some of those characteristics were touched on, but they deserve a more thorough review. After all, you're probably not trying to become a diamond expert but find the best-looking diamond for your future wife.

The factors that we will describe are fluorescence, brilliance and fire, and age. You'll probably remember brilliance and fire from the previous section. These factors will affect the value of a diamond very differently from the 4 C's. The effect they have on the diamond will be largely subjective and give each diamond its unique personality.

This isn't to say that they are arbitrarily assigned. Fluorescence in particular should be determined in a laboratory setting and is measured on a scale. Once you understand the basis for these factors, you will have a clear idea of what to look for. It is also possible to grade a diamond's fire by tracing the effect of light rays entering and exiting it, but this isn't commonly done.

Fluorescence

When exposed to ultraviolet rays, around 30% of diamonds will display some degree of fluorescence, meaning they will glow. The strength of a diamond's reaction to UV light is its fluorescence.

Most diamonds that fluoresce emit a blue/white light, but other colors may also appear on rare occasions. This phenomenon has to be exceptionally strong to affect appearance under normal conditions because the UV rays present in daylight are very weak. The fluorescence only affects a diamond's appearance to the untrained eye in about 10% of stones.

Strong fluorescence isn't necessarily a bad thing. It may even be the case that visible fluorescence makes a diamond more attractive to some. It will depend on the viewer and the other characteristics of the diamond. There's nothing about fluorescence levels that is inherently detrimental to the stone. Trace amounts of specific elements within the diamond cause this phenomenon. When UV light interacts with these elements, they glow.

Fluorescence will affect diamonds in different ways based on their color. For exceptionally clear diamonds graded D through H on the clarity scale, fluorescence is generally not wanted. For diamonds that are lower on the scale, it can provide a natural counterpoint to the yellow tint, thus making them appear clearer.

Not every dealer will give information about this factor, so you might have to ask for it specifically. Fluorescence is graded on a scale from None to Very Strong and it should have an effect on a stone's price.

The main reason to be concerned about a stone's fluorescence is to satisfy personal tastes. You could even ask to see the diamond under a UV light, but don't lose sleep over it.

Brilliance and Fire

In truth, the cut is the major determinant when it comes to brilliance and fire. You can think of brilliance as the way in which light reflects and refracts when hitting a diamond. To understand this better, let's take a step back.

When diamonds are processed and crafted from a rough gemstone, they undergo faceting. Facets are the sides of a diamond and they aren't made at random. The correct execution of the faceting process is what determines how light will bounce off the diamond. You can think of the facets as mirrors – when the light hits them at the right angle, they reflect or refract light. If the "mirrors" in a diamond are aligned perfectly, you get a much brighter stone.

This is why the cut is so important and you won't go wrong investing in a Very Good or Excellent graded diamond. If you look at two similar gems with different quality cuts, the effect will be readily apparent. A diamond's brilliance is largely the reason diamonds are so beautiful; no other stone appears quite so sparkly and bright. If the faceting is not done correctly, the brilliance and fire will appear chaotic and disjointed.

For many people, fire is the most attractive characteristic of diamonds. When white light hits a diamond just right, it acts as a prism, dispersing the light into distinct colors. These dancing flashes of color are called fire. This dispersion of light and the interplay of colors it creates are also the results of a quality cut. The light source and the position of the observer also play important roles but not as much as the cut.

The diamond's clarity will have a big impact on both the brilliance and the fire of the stone. Generally speaking, the lower the clarity, the less impressive these traits will be. Inclusions in and around areas where the light would break up impede its passing and reduce the sparkle.

Diamonds may not seem like they need all that much attention, but their appearance is very affected by neglect. Keeping a diamond clean of dust and grime will do wonders to enhance the natural fire that it produces.

Other factors, such as clarity, will also affect a diamond's brightness and fire but none so much as the cut. The type of light source also makes a difference, and you can expect a showroom to present diamonds in the best possible light. It's not unusual to ask to see a diamond under different light sources and you should do so if you want to make a fully informed purchase.

Age of Stone

Diamonds have been around for a long time. Even a "young" natural diamond is likely to be dated as well over a billion years old. It's fascinating to think that something formed so long ago now rests on someone's finger. Of course, for our purposes, we're not discussing the geological age of diamonds. As the saying goes, "diamonds are forever," and many diamonds on the market today were mined and cut hundreds of years ago.

Dating diamonds is an important consideration because it can have a significant impact on price. Any diamond crafted in the last two decades is probably laser-cut, or at least precision-machined. This makes them much more uniform but detracts from their character. Most diamonds sold today use the modern round brilliant cut. However, even before the advent of all the modern cutting technology, gem cutters were creating stunning diamonds by hand.

The oldest recognized cut that we still have in common circulation today is the old mine cut (OMC). This cut was very popular in the 1800s and good examples of it remain to this day. The term 'old mine' refers to the old mines of Brazil and India before Africa became the hotbed of diamond production it is today. An old mine cut has 58 facets, a number still used today in the round brilliant cut. The OMC produces a square-like stone with rounded corners.

Sometimes referred to as cushion cut, the unique charm of OMC diamonds is that they were measured and cut by hand. Even the best artisans in the world couldn't make two identical copies of a diamond by hand if they tried. This makes every OMC diamond distinctive —

there's no other like it. Knowing that you're getting something completely unique carries with it special romantic connotations.

Most old miners have been lost for a variety of reasons. Theft and destruction of property certainly account for a large number of the losses. But one very big reason is that they fell out of favor. When modern cuts became popular, many diamonds — especially high-quality ones — were recut to improve their marketability. Fortunately, that trend has reversed, and the subtle grace of old cut diamonds is prized today.

Given that the OMC diamonds were mined and produced so long ago, the environmental and social impacts of buying them today are virtually zero. If you're concerned about ethically sourced diamonds, old mine cuts have that covered.

They were also made before the era of grading systems and hyper commercialization. The attractiveness of a diamond was the chief goal. In the pursuit of that goal, gem cutters did everything in their power to make the most beautiful stone they could. If a stone wasn't attractive, clarity and carats were of little comfort.

The old mine cut is once again rising in popularity and some new diamonds are being cut in the old style today. If you want something a little more unique for your engagement ring, consider this type of cut. If you can't find a ring that you like with an OMC diamond, you may have better luck getting an unmounted stone. Speak with your jeweler about setting a diamond in a new mounting or updating the mounting of one that's already set.

The old European cut is another popular cut that was developed before modern cutting techniques. They were crafted roughly between 1890 and 1930. This cut is similar in appearance to the modern round brilliant cut with some important differences.

For one, the top facet in the old European cut tends to be much smaller and the bottom facet (culet) much larger.

The old European cut also tends to have much larger areas of light and dark which some people find appealing. If you're looking for this cut specifically, you'll be limited in your options, but a decent amount still remains.

It can be difficult to determine the exact age of a diamond. If you're dead set on looking for an antique stone, the cut of the stone is your main ally. These are the old diamond cuts still available today:

- Antique Emerald Cut
- Old European Cut
- Rose Cut Diamond
- Antique Oval and Marquise Cuts
- French Cut Diamond
- Antique Cushion Cut
- Antique Asscher Cut
- Old Mine Cut

You're not guaranteed an antique diamond if it has one of these cuts, but it increases the odds. Rather than learning all the differences between them, ask your jeweler about the cut and look for the ones on this list. On the other hand, some cuts, such as the round brilliant cut, are modern developments and will never appear in older stones.

Another important distinction of antique diamonds is the culet, or bottom facet. The bottom facet on modern cut diamonds is often too small for the naked eye to see. In antique diamonds, that kind of precision was not possible. If the culet is large enough to be visible, you're very likely dealing with an older diamond.

If you want to be as certain as you can, rely on a professional. There are many jewelers that specialize in certifying antique pieces. You can ask them to inspect the diamond and determine its age as accurately as possible. There are many more factors that they will take into account.

A GUIDE TO ENGAGEMENT RINGS

If you have the opportunity to do so, visit a store or gallery and ask to see some old cut diamonds. There's no substitute for seeing them in person, and you might just find yourself captivated by their beauty.

THE ANATOMY OF A RING

The best way to start your quest for the perfect engagement ring is to get familiar with the parts of a ring. The point of this section is not to pelt you with the terminology. You should try to get a sense of what you want in a ring when you start shopping. Knowing how to communicate that to your jeweler will help a lot.

If a ring was a movie, the director would be the center diamond. This is also called the 'feature stone' or 'primary stone'. It rests at the top of the ring and it's the largest stone in the ring. The first thing that draws the eye is the center diamond; everything else should be working to elevate it. Diamonds are the most common stones in engagement rings, but other gems are used as well.

Engagement rings will typically have either one or three stones. The center stone is sometimes flanked by two smaller stones. The function of the side stones is to accentuate the brilliance of the main diamond. Therefore, they are always smaller. The primary stone can also be surrounded by much smaller diamonds in what is known as a 'halo setting'.

The primary stone, as well as all other stones, are usually held in place by 'prongs.' The prongs are metal arms that secure the stones to the ring. Prongs are designed to be as unobtrusive as possible while still being suitable for their function. Another style of setting is the 'bezel'. It's less common than prongs and uses a metal rim to hide the lower half of the stones. The bezel is a more secure setting than prongs but leaves less of the diamond visible.

Moving down, the next part is the gallery. The area between the center stone and the rest of the ring is known as the gallery. Not all rings have a gallery and styles vary widely. Rings with halos don't usually have a gallery. If you're looking for a ring with an ornate gallery, it's best to stay away from halo settings. Galleries in antique rings were very prized and tend to be much more intricate than their modern counterparts.

The next part of the ring is the shoulders. This encompasses the top part of the band and is sized arbitrarily. Some rings have plain shoulders with no added work, while others have complex accents and gems. Choose a style of shoulders that is pleasing but doesn't detract from the primary stone.

The rest of the band that doesn't belong to the shoulders is called the shank. Shanks come in many varieties and each will suit a specific taste and stone. Shanks can also have engravings or filigree to enhance their appearance. Some common shank types for engagement rings include:

- The plain shank is a straight loop of precious metal. There is no tapering or splitting and it can have flat or rounded edges.

- A tapered shank gets thinner where it meets with the center stone and contributes to the apparent size of the diamond.
- Diamond studded shanks are exactly that, they can be completely or partially studded with diamonds.
- In split shanks, the band splits off into two as it meets the stone, giving the impression that there are two bands.
- Triple wire shanks are popular in vintage rings. They are made of three metal wires pressed together to add width.
- The bypass shank is less common but has a very distinctive look. The band in this type of shank doesn't meet in a straight line. Rather, it follows through the sides of the gem, overlapping itself.
- Cathedral shanks are very popular and can be considered a type of setting. In this type of shank, the sides extend upward to hold a gem rather than remaining separate from the prongs.

The setting design plays a key role in a ring's appearance. There are too many setting types to list, but you should be acquainted with some basic settings and their names. This way, you'll have a starting point to discuss an in-between setting style if none of them appeal to you.

- Solitaire Setting

Solitaire settings are the most popular types of engagement ring. They feature the primary stone, which is frequently held by prongs, and remove most other embellishments. A plain shank is usually preferred to further enhance the appearance of the center diamond. This type of setting is very good if you have an especially noteworthy diamond. It will allow a lot of light to hit the stone and give it the most attention. The drawback of this setting is that it sacrifices a lot of personality. A single stone on a plain shank may be impressive, but it doesn't say much about the wearer.

- Pavé Setting

The pavé setting is meant to help a diamond that doesn't draw the eye as much. This type of setting uses very small diamonds to cover large parts of the ring, giving the appearance of a large sparkling surface. It's very useful in enhancing the brilliance of a diamond and fits both vintage and modern styles. In some cases, the entire band may be covered in these small diamonds, but this will make resizing the ring difficult.

- Halo Setting

Halo settings were briefly introduced earlier, but they should be considered seriously as a way to make the most of your diamond. In the halo setting the center stone is surrounded by smaller stones, and this has a similar effect to the pavé setting. The halo can be customized to make the most out of the principal stone. For instance, a contrast can be created by using different types of stones in the halo. The halo will make a smaller stone appear larger but it will have an even more impressive effect on a larger diamond. A benefit of this style is that the stones in the halo will add some protection to the primary stone, but they can become loose themselves.

- Three-Stone Setting

Three-stone settings are another good way to incorporate different colored gemstones into your ring to great effect. This type of setting is different from the halo or pavé setting in that it uses three larger stones instead of one. The romantic implication is that the three stones represent the couple's past, present, and future. When selecting the types of stone, three diamonds are a safe bet. Different colored stones can be very beautiful, but you run the risk of pairing them in a way that detracts from the primary stone.

- Vintage Setting

Vintage settings are the best way to add character to your ring. There isn't a specific way to describe a vintage or antique setting. Vintage rings followed the styles of the time, but the types of embellishments and ornaments used were so varied that they're hard to classify. Vintage rings will be discussed in detail in a later section. For now, keep in mind that every vintage ring you see will probably be somewhat unique, so it's worth shopping around and seeing a lot of them in person.

Another crucial part of a ring is the accenting stones. This is an umbrella term that refers to all the diamonds that aren't the center diamond. A ring can have as many or as few accenting stones as the craftsman wants to add. The halo, shoulder stones, gallery stones, and stones on the shank are all accent stones.

Accenting stones are a special breed of stone and they're usually cut for their specific purpose. They usually have fewer facets, so they don't compete for attention with the center diamond. They also have a lower color grade as they're very small and harder to discern. Typically, accent stones don't go past 0.25 carats (twenty-five pointers) and stay in the 0.10-carat region.

Finally, every ring has its own distinctive hallmarks. These are the markings on the ring that communicate things like who made it, the quality of the metal used, and other such details. Other common markings include the country of origin, the carat weight of the center diamond, and any custom engraving that you'd like added. Having a custom engraving is a great way to add a personal touch to your engagement ring.

Those are the basic parts of any engagement ring. There are other parts that will be specific to particular settings and styles, but these will be enough to have a productive conversation with your jeweler.

Remember that, in a sense, everything revolves around the center diamond. You never want to place a stone in a setting that will detract from its qualities. The beauty of a ring is a matter of taste, but don't hesitate to ask about the best settings for particular stones.

WHAT IS THE KIMBERLEY PROCESS?

Natural resources have always been among the biggest causes of human conflict. Diamonds are no different. They are a very valuable commodity and have been used to fund conflicts around the globe. These "conflict diamonds" are extracted using unsustainable mining practices in parts of the world where civil instability is high. When this kind of exploitation reached a critical point, states and the diamond industry were forced to take action.

Diamonds are not the only resource to be used in this manner, but their high value and abundance in very vulnerable areas of the world make them a special case. The gravity of the situation was first brought to the public eye in 1998. An organization called Global Witness published a report tracking the funding of conflict in some African nations to rough diamonds. The report also showed how governments and companies were complicit in this trade (knowingly or not).

The Global Witness report, as well as other reports that followed, mobilized many of the key players in the diamond trade, who in turn put a system into place which could regulate the trade of rough diamonds to avoid funding war efforts. The main concerns were — and continue to be — the funding of illegitimate political goals and the brutal conditions used to extract the diamonds. Early efforts included the United Nations resolution 1173 to impose sanctions on conflict areas.

The initial resolution was meant to be a starting point, and it soon became clear that it wasn't doing enough. In May 2000, the UN Security Council met in Kimberley, South Africa to decide on a method that would bring this diamond trade to an end. There was a lot of concern about the impact any method would have on legitimate diamond trade, but the situation had become critical.

In September 2000, the Kimberley Process Certification Scheme (KPCS) was created following the meeting in Kimberley. By 2003, the Kimberley Process received full support from the United Nations and has been in effect ever since.

Today, the Kimberley Process has 54 participants, which represent 81 countries. The Kimberley Process is credited with all but eradicating conflict diamond trade. Companies and entities in the diamond industry don't receive membership to the scheme, but they have largely implemented systems of self-regulation. If a diamond can't be tracked to a Kimberley-compliant source, it will be unsellable in the broader market.

The Kimberley Process starts on the level of legislation. Member nations are expected to enter into law certain regulations regarding the import and export of diamonds. These legislative requirements must meet the criteria established by the certification scheme. The members also commit to using transparent practices in tracing the source of diamonds and to making all relevant data available.

Kimberley Process members commit to engaging in rough diamond trade only with other member states. This makes it difficult for any country relying on the diamond trade for its revenue to remain outside the certification. Finally, a system of warranties is implemented when transporting diamonds. The warranty compels all diamond traders to make and (if requested) provide proof of the following statement:

"The diamonds herein invoiced have been purchased from legitimate sources not involved in funding conflict and in compliance with United Nations resolutions. The seller hereby guarantees that these diamonds are conflict-free, based on personal knowledge and/or written guarantees provided by the supplier of these diamonds."

This certification process wouldn't be possible without the voluntary involvement of the diamond industry. Several industry organizations have drafted a set of self-regulatory principles to accommodate the process. These principles revolve around the commitment to buying only diamonds from sources that voluntarily comply with the KPCS.

The Kimberley Process has been important in reducing the trade of conflict diamonds worldwide, but it has received criticism as well. Many organizations think that the process doesn't do enough. In fact, Global Witness — the organization largely responsible for exposing conflict diamonds — left the scheme in 2011 claiming it had failed to meet the established goals.

A large part of the criticism stemmed from the certification of diamond fields seized by force in Zimbabwe. Several of the key people in establishing the process have since walked away in protest and seeing as the credibility of the process is what makes it possible, any doubts about the intentions of the KPCS are devastating to its reputation. Proposals to replace it have been made but, as it stands, it is still the best solution so far.

It's not a perfect answer to the problem, and efforts are continuing in trying to refine the process. However, it has produced an undeniably positive effect. Most serious jewelers recognize the Kimberley Process as a valuable tool and stand ready to support any efforts to ethically source diamonds.

As a buyer, you're entitled to know that your purchase doesn't compromise the livelihood and integrity of other people. Asking for proof that the diamonds you buy are responsibly sourced is perfectly reasonable. At Estate Diamond Jewelers, we take pride in making sure every measure is taken in establishing the ethical source of our diamonds. Any doubts regarding the credibility of a diamond's origin will result in our refusal to buy and market it.

This is where the use and sale of old diamonds makes a huge difference. By using vintage stones whose origins can be established reliably, you won't be contributing to the further encroachment of human rights. Some argue that enough diamonds have been extracted to fulfill the demands for jewelry into perpetuity. This is likely not true, but the fact remains that buying old diamonds is the only way to guarantee an ethical purchase.

UNDERSTANDING VINTAGE RINGS

We covered vintage ring styles in an earlier chapter, but they deserve an in-depth look. Vintage jewelry has slowly but surely made a comeback in recent years. The minimalist and functional designs of modern jewelry were very popular in the 1990s. At that point, jewelry served as a status symbol as much as an individual statement.

The resurgence in demand for older jewelry in the past 10–15 years can be linked to a number of trends. For one, new designers have been entering the scene wanting to make their mark. New trends in design provided people a larger variety of options. Independent crafters also entered the scene and jewelry returned to its 19th-century roots where women saw rings as an expression of individuality.

With this shift, rings became more personalized and the interest for vintage rings soared. Vintage rings, and antique rings for that matter, tend to have much more personality than modern pieces. This makes them better suited for the new trends in ring buying. Buyers want to feel that their ring is not just part of a series, and a handcrafted ring gives the wearer a sense of ownership that they wouldn't otherwise have.

The diversity of styles and motifs from the late 19th and early 20th centuries offer women the chance to stand out and express their identity in their jewelry again. All these factors coupled with the free access to information via the internet created the perfect conditions for the revival of the vintage ring market. Last, but not least, sustainability is built-in to true vintage pieces. Purchasing an estate ring is guaranteed to create no additional impact.

Unfortunately, the popularity of vintage rings hasn't translated into a better understanding of what they are. If you are trying to find a vintage ring, you should get acquainted with the terminology. It will help you in several ways. All the information you find, whether online or in stores, will be confusing if you don't know the basic elements.

Another important advantage is that you will save money by not overpaying for something that you don't want or need. Also, if you know the terminology going in, you'll be able to recognize when it's not used correctly. If you recognize that a jeweler is misusing certain terms, you can assume a lack of education or potential dishonesty. It will also help give you confidence in your purchase.

Vintage, Estate, and Antique Jewelry

The best place to start is to establish the difference between these three terms. The term 'vintage' is used interchangeably with the term 'antique' by some jewelers, but this isn't accurate. A vintage ring is any ring older than 20 years. When people say vintage, they are talking about rings made after the 1930s — retro era, Art Deco, and Hollywood-inspired 1940s rings are all vintage.

The term vintage doesn't describe a design movement or artistic preferences, but rather is defined by age. Given this, rings that fall into the vintage category today will become antiques in the future, and modern rings will become vintage. Keep this in mind as you look for a ring; the term vintage encompasses many different designs and styles.

Antique rings, on the other hand, are over 100 years old. The terms are not used with exact precision and some jewelers will refer to anything over 80 years old as antique. Again, antique refers to a time period, not a style. Victorian and Edwardian styles fall into the antique category at this point and they're currently very popular.

The last of these terms, 'estate', simply describes jewelry that has been previously owned. Any antique or vintage ring that you find in a store is estate jewelry. Estate doesn't relate to a style or time period, but rather ownership. Any piece of jewelry that isn't brand new falls into this category.

Those are the three primary terms relating to older rings. Another useful one to know is period style jewelry. Period style rings incorporate antique diamonds, such as old mine and European cut diamonds, in new settings. These settings are often inspired by vintage and antique design styles.

Given the limited availability of vintage rings, a period style ring is a good option if you can't find something you really like. Keep in mind that the craftsmanship in vintage rings will generally be of very high quality. Replicating that skill and attention to detail could come with a hefty price tag.

Other Considerations

When you're buying an antique or vintage ring, keep in mind that it has stood the test of time. Their delicate decorations are obviously durable, but they should be looked after with special care. This is especially true of the flowery Victorian ring design. It's not uncommon for vintage rings to need repairs at some point. Ask your jeweler if the ring has been repaired in the past. Even if they weren't then ones to repair it, they might have records of any repairs done.

Also, keep in mind that the stones used in older rings won't be of the same quality as a modern diamond. It was discussed in the section on types of cuts, and it bears repeating. Diamonds cut by hand won't have the precision that's available today and could be a little less bright in some cases. Some impurities were also impossible to detect without modern methods.

The best way to get acquainted with all the different cuts, shapes, and styles is to shop around at reputable dealers. There is so much variety in vintage and antique rings that you'll easily find one that perfectly suits your girlfriend's tastes. When buying any jewelry — particularly vintage jewelry — it's important to develop trust in the people you're buying from. You'll have to rely on the experience of specialists to get a truly beautiful piece that is worth what you pay for it.

HOW TO SAVE MONEY ON YOUR ENGAGEMENT RING

Getting engaged is the first step towards building a shared future with your partner. In a perfect world, you would enjoy decades of a wonderful union and support each other through thick and thin. There's little point in starting this union by acquiring debt. Engagement rings are an important traditional detail, but they are hardly a priority if you're having financial difficulties.

If you approach the buying process with the right method and mindset, you'll be surprised at the results. Understanding all the key aspects of diamond grading is only the beginning. When the time comes to put your money where your research is, you'll be happy that you invested the time and effort into learning about rings.

There are a lot of strategic ways to save money on your ring without sacrificing quality to any great degree. You probably picked up on some of them as you were reading through this chapter. There are a few more methods which are less obvious. For the sake of clarity, this section will have a summary of all the best ways to save when buying a ring.

Before you even begin to look for a ring, consider your budget. In the section on choosing the right amount to spend, you'll find many good ways to approach this matter. Once you have a budget in mind, you can reduce the number of options drastically.

Pick the right setting for your stone

Invest some time into learning about the different types of settings. A big part of ring design is getting the most apparent size out of the least amount of diamond. A halo setting, for instance, gives the impression that the primary stone is much larger than what is actually on the ring.

Halo settings were very common in earlier time periods. An added benefit is that it will give your ring a vintage look even if it isn't actually vintage. Most of the cost-saving measures will revolve around spending less on the stone itself, so start with this one.

Stay away from the "magic sizes"

Diamond carat weight has a massive impact on its price, but the price changes drastically at the half-carat and one-carat sizes. For some reason, round numbers carry a premium. Think of turning 18 years old and suddenly you can vote and buy property, but nothing significant changes from turning 17. Similarly, a few carat points don't make a visible difference on the diamond.

Buying just shy of these sizes will reduce the cost without having an impact on the appearance. Try to find diamonds that are .91 to .99 carats for the visual appeal of a one-carat gem without the price tag.

Never buy from chain jewelers

A chain jeweler at a shopping center can be a good place to learn about diamonds and rings. The people working there will generally be knowledgeable and they will have a decent selection of modern jewelry to look at. When it comes to buying from these places, you're better off avoiding it.

Chain jewelers spend a lot of money on advertising to build an image and give their customers confidence. However, the rent they are paying is usually sky-high. Those expenses have to be passed on somehow, and it will end up in the ring prices. This instantly puts you at a disadvantage because you're paying for overhead rather than ring value.

Remember that color is relative.

The color scale should be understood in context. First of all, minute differences in color are hard to notice even for experts. Getting a J-graded diamond is perfectly fine as long as the tint isn't obvious, though you shouldn't go much lower. Keep in mind that the stone will always appear on a ring.

A diamond may be graded very low and still look clear in the right setting. A halo of darker stones or a yellow gold band can help a stone with a light tint seem much clearer. If you're choosing an unmounted diamond, take this into consideration and try to see a similar diamond in a setting you like to have a point of reference.

A GUIDE TO ENGAGEMENT RINGS

Try to buy a set

If you're in the market for an engagement ring, chances are you'll be looking for wedding bands soon as well. If you're in a position to do so, try to buy all of them at once (or from the same seller). There's a good chance that you can negotiate a better deal by spending a little more, which segues neatly into the next point.

Learn to negotiate

You want to buy a ring and the jeweler wants to sell it to you. With this in mind there's nothing wrong with trying to reach a price that you can both live with. This will only happen in a brick-and-mortar showroom, which you should make every attempt to visit.

Don't think of buying a ring like walking into a supermarket and picking up fruit. Try to think of it like buying a car, where you want the right combination of characteristics. That said, jewelers aren't car dealers, so don't expect to bully them in a negotiation. Some independent dealers simply won't negotiate, and that's perfectly fine too if their prices meet your budget.

Save money on the metal

Engagement rings are very commonly made of platinum. It's a very durable metal with a naturally white color that doesn't dull. It's ideal for engagement rings for a lot of reasons, but it's also very expensive. The price of platinum by weight is actually quite similar to gold, but it's much denser. This means that more platinum is needed to make a ring.

A good way to save with very little downside is opting for a gold or white gold ring. White gold is plated with rhodium and will have to be replated eventually, but it's worth considering over platinum. Of course, if you were looking for a gold ring anyway, you might consider a palladium band, but you'll have trouble finding any vintage rings made out of palladium.

One thing to consider is allergies. Platinum is the best option for someone prone to allergic reactions.

Get a clear picture of the clarity

Much like the color, clarity is important to the price of a diamond, but it's not as important to the appearance. Make no mistake, large leaps in clarity will be noticeable, but every diamond is different. Clarity defines the degree to which a diamond contains imperfections, but these imperfections affect each stone differently.

What you want to look for is an "eye clean" diamond. Forget about the clarity grade — if you can't see any imperfections with the naked eye, it's good enough. However, you should keep in mind that you need to know what you're looking for. Ask your jeweler to show you what a heavily included diamond looks like and what a difference in clarity this makes.

Choose prongs over a bezel

A bezel setting encases the stone in metal, making a tight and secure fit. It's great for active people because the diamond isn't as exposed and the tighter grip will prevent it from coming loose. The downside is that it requires more metal and is therefore more expensive.

Prongs hold the stone on a few points, but they display more of it.

A prong setting requires a little more care but not to an unreasonable degree. A little bit of caution is a decent trade off to reduce the price.

Think outside the diamond

This one is a bit of a risk, and it only comes into play if you're on a very tight budget. The conventional wisdom is that diamonds are used in engagement rings. That might seem arbitrary, but it's how people perceive them. Of course, that's like saying money can't buy happiness. If you believe that, why are you looking for an engagement ring? The truth is that money can buy happiness and engagement rings don't absolutely need diamonds.

If your girlfriend is truly okay with it — or if you intend to replace the stone later — don't be afraid to look for another type of gem. Keep in mind that diamonds are so popular because of their appearance and their durability. Other stones will be more fragile. For instance, a ruby with diamond accents can make a stunning ring for a fraction of the price.

Don't mess with the cut

This isn't so much of a recommendation on where to save as a recommendation on how to focus your budget. The most important factor when it comes to a diamond's overall appearance is the quality of the cut. A very good cut will trump clarity, color, and weight, so don't be afraid to give priority to the cut over the rest. In short, buy the best cut you can afford and save money in other areas.

Use pavé diamonds for a bigger impact

An important factor for any ring is how impressive it looks when it's worn. You'll often find that a smaller primary stone with abundant accents makes a bigger impression than a lone diamond. This is where pavé diamonds excel.

These tiny diamonds (commonly around 0.10 carats) "pave" the band of a ring and increase its brilliance and sparkle. You can get away with a smaller center diamond and a band covered in pavé diamonds. Because of their small size and frequently lower quality, they tend to be fairly inexpensive, but their effect is enormous. When shopping around, try to look at many rings with a pavé setting; you'll be impressed at how big of a difference they make.

Buy your ring online

While you should definitely see many rings in person, when it comes time to buy, you'll probably find better prices online. You should try to not buy a ring unseen, or if you do, make sure there is an airtight return policy.

Many independent dealers will have physical locations as well as websites, so you can ask to see a ring you found online in person. Online prices will usually be better, and if you look out for promotional discounts, you can easily save a lot of money.

Reuse a setting or stone that you already own

The best way to reduce the price of your ring is to not buy it, in a sense. If you have a ring or a gem that you are particularly fond of —

such as a family heirloom — give it new life by upcycling it.

A beautiful antique band with a new modern cut diamond can be extremely beautiful. Similarly, an older diamond with a high-quality vintage cut mounted into a new ring works just as well. You also get to preserve a piece of family history in the process.

That should give you plenty of avenues to take when trying to choose an affordable ring. All of these are valid methods, and it pays to be thrifty, but remember that you're trying to make a statement. If you're buying a ring at all, you should try to make it the best ring you can comfortably afford.

No one should put themselves into financial trouble over an engagement ring — doing so would defeat the purpose entirely. Take the time to learn all about selecting diamonds and rings and then apply that knowledge to get the best deal you can.

CHAPTER 4
HOW TO PROPOSE

The moment of truth has finally arrived. You've found your person, and the only thing that remains is to make sure you're her person too. You probably have a slew of scenarios running through your head, most of which involve some variation of you on one bent knee. If you're excited and jittery at the prospect of proposing, you're doing it right.

It's important to not let your anxiety get the best of you. If you're thinking about proposing, then it probably won't be a complete surprise when you do. You would have at least discussed it with your partner, or you've been together long enough that it feels like the natural progression for both of you. Calm your nerves and steel your resolve because we're going to jump right into the dreaded face-to-face conversation with your future father-in-law.

ASKING PERMISSION FROM HER FATHER

The tradition of asking for a girl's hand in marriage is much less common than it once was. Especially in Western societies, it's seen as an outdated practice for many reasons. That's why it will be that much more impactful and meaningful when you do it. Most women and parents will probably see it as a very thoughtful gesture.

While you would traditionally ask your girlfriend's father for his blessing, it's acceptable to ask her mother. If her father has passed away or otherwise isn't present in her life, speak with her mother instead. Having said that, if she's not close to either of her parents, it may be better to avoid asking altogether.

Ideally, you will already have established a relationship with her parents. If it's going to be the first time you speak with her dad, it might make things a bit awkward because you have to get through the initial pleasantries. If her parents don't live nearby, plan to have the conversation at their next family gathering.

The best way to approach the conversation would be to arrange a social situation where you can be with her father alone. A meal somewhere would be ideal, but an intimate conversation at home works just as well. When you ask to speak with him, there's no reason to be completely candid about the reason, but don't be secretive either. In all likelihood, he will suspect what it's about and you can proceed naturally.

The first part of the conversation should be about your feelings for his daughter. Talk about all the reasons why you make a good match and why you feel it's time to take the next step in your relationship. Once you've established how you feel, get to the point and tell him you want to marry his daughter. Most fathers will appreciate hearing about how dedicated you are to making their daughter happy and the lifelong commitment you intend to make.

There's no reason to make this an hour-long dissertation — deliver your message seriously and succinctly with conviction. Once the cards are on the table, ask for his blessing to go through with the proposal. If you've done your due diligence, you'll leave with his blessing and a renewed sense of commitment to your relationship.

TOP 99 PROPOSAL IDEAS

When planning your proposal, you want everything to be just right. After all, you want a marriage that will last a lifetime, so it should start with a beautiful memory. Think for a second about what it means to propose — that is, what it is you are proposing. The proposition is that a person will be better off with you than with anyone else on earth. Honor that idea by making your proposal truly unforgettable.

Only a professional planner has the wherewithal to plan a fairy tale proposal in a week. Unless you fit into that category, give yourself some time to create the conditions that are necessary to pull off your idea. There's always the danger of something going wrong and foiling your proposal, but the bigger issue is showing that you put in the effort that the occasion demands.

Remember that this isn't all about you. You should feel like you're doing something special for your significant other. If this means going outside of your comfort zone, then so be it. Start by asking yourself some basic questions: Does she want a public proposal? Should it be a grand gesture or an intimate affair? Whatever you decide to do, keep in mind that you want to cherish this memory forever, so enlist the aid of a friend or professional to record the occasion.

Your biggest ally will be an attention to details. Things like where you first met, where you first kissed, and her favorite book will all be useful in planning your proposal. It's a good idea to have a short speech prepared, but don't overthink it. A few sentences about what you love about her and how much she means to you are enough. When you're ready to start planning, take a look at these proposal ideas to help you get started.

1. A quiet dinner. Restaurants are the classic proposal locale. Pick a place that you both love or one that is known for its romantic atmosphere. It's a good idea to make the staff aware of your plans ahead of time so there are no misunderstandings. They will also be able to help you make good decisions about seating and other arrangements. All that's left is to pick a natural place in the conversation to pop the question.
2. Write a love song. If you're musically inclined, this is an especially good idea, but it will make for a great proposal even if you're not. Put together a few verses and either hire a musician to set them to music or sing them a cappella. Don't worry about your singing voice, she will love it.
3. Propose in a photo booth. There's an old-fashioned charm to photo booths that's difficult to replicate. Not too many venues have them these days, so it'll take a bit of searching. Take the ring with you into the booth and ask her between shots to record her genuine reaction.
4. Pick her up at the airport. The next time you need to pick her up at the airport, receive her with a sign that says "Mrs." followed by your last name. She'll realize what's going on immediately and it will make her arrival that much better.
5. Make a personalized jigsaw puzzle. This option works best if your girlfriend loves puzzles to begin with. Pick one of the many online services that create personalized jigsaw puzzles and have them make one for your proposal. Use a picture of the two of you with "Will you marry me?" overlaid.
6. A romantic getaway. This is a popular option for good reason. It takes a little more planning than others, but it is well worth it. Take

a vacation with her and propose when you arrive to have a break and a celebration all in one.
7. Propose at a concert. Get tickets to see her favorite band. Proposing during her favorite song is a foolproof way to get a 'yes'. If you want to go the extra mile, talk to the venue's management to see if the band would agree to dedicate the song to you and her.
8. Recreate your first date. Be as detailed as you can be with this proposal. Try to remember the music that was playing, the food you ordered, and what you wore. If it's still a place you frequent as a couple, she won't even suspect it by the time you ask her.
9. A magical proposal at Disney. The timeless magic of Disney parks makes a great place for proposing. You'll probably be there the entire day, so you'll have plenty of good opportunities. Many proposals take place at Disney, so talk to the staff in advance and they'll help you make the perfect plan.
10. Make a website. If you're good on the computer, use a hosting service to create a proposal website. It's a wonderful gesture that she can easily share with her friends and family. You can get really creative with this. For instance, make an online photo album of the two of you.
11. Propose under fireworks. Fireworks are a great thematic component to illustrate the feelings between you. If you go with this option, be sure to hire a professional photographer who can capture the glorious backdrop.
12. Propose while she sleeps. Carefully slip the ring on her finger while she is sleeping, then wait for the confused look when she wakes up. Bring her breakfast in bed the next day to make it extra special.
13. Propose at an outdoor screening. Plan a romantic picnic at an outdoor screening of her favorite movie. If the movie happens to be romantic, all the better. Look for a break in the action to get the ring and ask her.
14. New Year's Eve proposal. You'll be in a festive mood and the atmosphere will already be charged. New Year's is the perfect stage for

a proposal. Propose during the countdown for a truly happy new year — and many more to come.
15. Get help from a pet. Putting your ring on your pet's collar is another sweet way to surprise her. If you don't have pets, what better way to mark the occasion than by adopting one?
16. Make an artistic proposal. Enlist the help of a local art gallery for this one. Make a piece that they will agree to display for you and visit the art gallery together. For example, you can create a painting of the words "Will you marry me?" Make sure it's clear that the piece was made by you and present her with the ring when she sees it.
17. Hot air balloon ride. Proposing in the clouds is another timeless tradition. When scheduling your ride, discuss your plan with the service operator so the pilot is notified. Most pilots won't have any issues with taking a few pictures while you're in the air and you can have a photographer waiting for you at the bottom.
18. Propose during trivia night. A great idea for trivia-loving couples. The next time you go to a trivia night, discreetly speak with the emcee to help you formulate the question. Then, just wait for it with your ring at the ready. A trivia night at home with friends will work just as well.
19. Propose at a sporting event. Most stadiums offer marriage proposal arrangements that can be made ahead of time. If you both have a favorite team, most big events have a system in place to assist you. Prices will vary a lot, so contact the team's management well before the date.
20. Make a themed proposal. Her favorite show, movie, or book makes for a great proposal setting. You can incorporate any number of elements into your proposal. Dress the part, have some themed music playing, and make her feel like she's a character in that world. Pick a special place for the two of you and enlist the help of friends to bring her there.
21. Take an art class. Pottery and painting classes for couples are easy to find. Take her to a class and pretend to work along with the in-

structor, but don't let her see your work. When it's time for the big reveal, show her the proposal-themed work that you have made while she was following the class.

22. Take her to the Queen of the Adriatic. Venice is one of the most romantic cities in Europe and an ideal place to propose. Consider hiring a gondola ride for just the two of you. Discuss your plans with the gondolier beforehand. He will probably have some good tips for the best point during the ride to pop the question.
23. Re-label her favorite food or drink. Whether she's an ice cream or wine lover, print customized labels with your proposal and replace them on the items. If you have several items, you can also make a series of cryptic messages. Be sure to have the ring nearby for when she discovers what's going on.
24. Ask her on a hike. Nature is the classic setting for just about anything you can imagine. Plan a hike with her and set up signs along the road beforehand. Start with something mysterious that makes her want to find the next sign in the series.
25. A beach proposal. Beach proposals offer a lot of variety. It can be something as simple as a stroll on your favorite beach or as complex as an oceanside table with live music. The serenity of the waves makes for a wonderful setting.
26. Propose in a rowboat. You should have the fundamentals of rowing down before you attempt this one. You don't need to own a rowboat, though. Most places with scenic lakes will offer rowboat or pedal boat rides. Also, consider a canoe ride through a state park for the perfect setting. Make sure to have the ring secured before you head out.
27. Top of the Empire State Building. The New York skyline has long been a favorite backdrop for couples. Professional photography is usually not allowed at the top, so make arrangements beforehand. The view is truly breathtaking, so take her breath away again by

presenting her with an engagement ring.

28. Play your song when she least expects it. This is a simple idea that can apply to just about any location. If you have a favorite song as a couple, that's perfect. Otherwise, pick her favorite song and surprise her by playing it at a completely unexpected place. You can enlist the help of the location's management or strategically hide a portable radio. Make a comment about how fitting the coincidence is because you've been meaning to ask her something.

29. Crash her night out. This will require the help of her friends. Have them plan a girls' night out and make sure they know when you will be coming. Alternatively, have them end up at a place where you will be waiting.

30. A dinner just for the two of you. If you have a favorite hole in the wall that you visit together, see about hiring out the entire place for an evening. The moment of surprise when she sees a completely empty place will be the right time to show her the ring. In this case, try to ask her before dinner starts so you can use it as a celebration.

31. Propose at an ice rink. Any ice rink will do, but the ice rink at Rockefeller Center goes the extra mile. Most outdoor rinks will be able to accommodate you and clear out the rink just for the two of you. Outdoor locations work better — nothing spells romance like a snow-covered proposal.

32. Plan out a scavenger hunt. To execute a good scavenger hunt, you're going to need help. Recruit your friends and family for ideas and help to deliver clues. Start by considering the end location and work backward from there, trying to use places and people who are meaningful for her. Don't make it obvious what the scavenger hunt is about at first. Instead, let her work it out along the way.

33. Propose from the sidelines of a merry-go-round. Doing this at an established park will allow you to plan better than a traveling fair that's only stopping by in your city. Make an excuse about why you

can't join her and have a series of placards ready to spell the words one by one as she goes around.
34. Turn your house or apartment into a photo album. Collect as many photos as you can of the two of you and stage your place to be a gallery dedicated to your relationship. Wait for her to arrive with the ring at the ready when she walks through the door.
35. Get some help from the little ones. If you have kids, they are the perfect allies for a proposal. You can also get some help from nieces and nephews. Get as creative as you like with this proposal — anything from a hand-delivered message to a poem recited by the kids will work wonderfully.
36. Drone-delivered proposal. A nice touch for outdoor proposals. Have a friend deliver your ring with a drone at a special location. You could also deliver the proposal yourself when she least expects it. If she typically has lunch outside, this will make for an unforgettable gesture.
37. Bridge the gap. Bridges are a great way to establish a metaphorical bond. Proposing on a bridge or near a famous bridge will send the message that you're committed to each other. When it comes to landmark bridges, you won't have to look far. You can even plan a vacation around it to explore a new city.
38. Write your proposal in the sky. Skywriting never goes out of style, but it can be tricky. Environmental factors such as wind conditions will play a huge role, so plan accordingly. Come up with a short and clear message that makes it obvious you are proposing. When it's time, make sure she's in a position to see it and draw her attention to the sky.
39. Make a custom fortune cookie. It's easy to find personalization services for just about anything these days, including fortune cookies. Have them put your proposal in the cookie's message and smuggle it in the next time you have Chinese food.

40. Take a wine cellar tour. Wine cellars have an air of excitement and mystery that creates a wonderful counterpoint for a proposal. You can arrange for a special event with the management or simply get on one knee while you're touring the cellar.
41. Commission a street art mural. You'll need to find a place that agrees to have someone paint on their wall, but the effort will be worth it. If you feel confident doing it yourself, take the plunge. Otherwise, hire a professional artist to make a mural that expresses your love and devotion.
42. Spell it really far away. A nature hike is the best way to pull this off. Bring some binoculars and have your friends hold up large signs in the distance spelling out the proposal. Pretend to notice something and ask her to help you figure out what it is. While she's looking through the binoculars, display the ring for her to see when she lowers them.
43. Print out customized t-shirts. Plan a gathering for your friends and family and print our customized t-shirts for everyone. The t-shirts should spell out the proposal and you can let her slowly realize what's going on. Make sure everyone arrives together and that you're wearing the one that says "me?"
44. Propose underwater. Scuba divers will especially love this idea. Have your dive shop help with the arrangements. Prepare an underwater sign, or just write the proposal on an underwater board. When she sees it, have the ring ready to go. Make sure the ring is securely attached to you to avoid spending more time underwater than you bargained for.
45. Make a comic book. A terrific idea for comic book lovers. If you're an artist, you can take matters into your own hands, but you can also find a comic book artist online. Design and print a unique proposal comic book and give it to her when she least expects it.
46. Get a personalized mug. Get her a custom mug with your proposal written on the bottom. When you're ready to propose, have a cup

of coffee with her and wait for her to finish hers. You may need to help her a bit if she doesn't see it at first.

47. A proposal in a bottle. A message in a bottle is a classic theme and you can get really creative with it. Put your proposal in a bottle and tie an anchor to it, then drop it in a lake or stream. When she sees it, you can have fun trying to retrieve it and witnessing the surprise when she sees the message is for her.

48. Stage a caricature proposal. Find a caricature artist that frequents an area you both visit. Speak with them beforehand about your plan and have them draw you proposing. When you suggest that you get a drawing made of the two of you together, she won't suspect a thing.

49. Replace the parts in your favorite board game. Whether you like simple games like Monopoly and Scrabble or more involved games, you will find plenty of ways to incorporate this idea. Make some custom replacements for cards or chips with your proposal on them, then play the game and wait for her to find the surprise.

50. Write it in the sand. This is a variation of the beach proposal which works best on beaches with a scenic overlook. Write your proposal in giant letters on the sand and take her for a stroll.

51. Propose in Morse code. Write your proposal on a piece of paper in Morse code, then mix it in with the mail. Act as surprised as she is when she notices and suggest that you decode it together.

52. Make a proposal flipbook. Flipbooks are easy to make and you can find detailed tutorials online. Consider coming up with a simple storyline that leads to a ring and illustrate it in a flipbook. Place the actual ring on the last page of the flipbook, but make sure she doesn't open that one first.

53. Propose on a dinner check. Sometimes the simplest surprises are the most effective. Make reservations at a nice restaurant and arrange for the waiter to add an item to the check that says "Will you marry me?" or something similar. When you're done with dinner,

pretend there's been a mistake and ask her to examine the check.
54. Propose in a tweet from her favorite celebrity. You'll have to be ingenious and persistent for this to work. If you can strike the right chord with the right celebrity, they might just tweet your proposal for you. There's no way to tell if or when it might happen, so be ready to jump into action at any time.
55. Geocache your proposal. Geocaching is a fun activity that involves hiding secret stashes at specific GPS coordinates. Take her on a geocaching date and hide your proposal in one of the caches. Arrange for the photographer to meet you at the site and try to make it near a nice restaurant for a celebratory meal.
56. Pop the question on an amusement park ride. Plan a visit to an amusement park and go on one of the rides that take your picture at the climax. Bring a concealed sign with you on the ride and hold it up to the camera at the right time. You should try to make it a ride that you've been on before so you know the exact moment when the picture is taken.
57. Hire a musician, or four. A good barbershop quartet will be able to help you put together a song for the occasion. Make all the arrangements and have them meet you at your proposal location. When they finish the song, join them on one knee and ask her to be your wife.
58. Record a hit single. If she's a vinyl lover, this proposal will make her swoon. Record a simple proposal or a song, or both! Use an online service to make a personalized vinyl record of your message.
59. Write your proposal in lights. This works best during the winter, but it can be used any time of year. When you're putting up decorations, spell out the message on your house. You could also just spell it out indoors and turn off all the lights for a magical surprise.
60. Propose with a scrapbook. Scrapbooks make for a great gift and show a lot of dedication and attention to detail. Put together a scrapbook with your best memories and gift it to her. The last page

of the book should have your ring and a simple question.
61. Fall behind during a walk. Another very simple proposal idea that has a big surprise element. Hide a sign with your proposal along a nature trail or walkway. When you take her for a walk, lag behind discreetly and grab your sign. By the time she notices and turns around, you'll be holding up the sign in one hand and the ring in the other.
62. Propose at a convention. For couples who like conventions, this is sure to be a treasured memory. If you're polite and resourceful, you could even get help from a celebrity attendee. Most celebrities at conventions will be happy to accommodate you within reason, but don't be too pushy.
63. Predict her fate. For this proposal idea, you will need a cooperative fortune teller or palm reader. Talk to the fortune teller beforehand and have them help you formulate the proposal. Take her to have her fortune read, and when the fortune teller predicts her marriage to you, seize the moment.
64. A grand proposal at the Grand Canyon. The majesty of the Grand Canyon is unmatched anywhere in the world. Planning a trip to see it is a perfect opportunity to take advantage of the awe-inspiring scenery. Contact local photographers before you go so you don't have to waste time when you arrive.
65. Propose in a helicopter. A helicopter ride is a wonderful way to spend an afternoon and an even better way to propose. Pop the question in mid-air and have your friends and family waiting for you when you land.
66. Propose next to her favorite animal. Whether she loves penguins or pandas, chances are a zoo or aquarium nearby has a program to let you see them up close. Take her to see her favorite animal and produce the ring while she's interacting with them.
67. Propose in her favorite book. Get a copy of her favorite book or two copies of a book she's been wanting to read. Hollow out a space

in the pages of the book to fit your ring and proposal. Regrettably, the book will be illegible, but it will serve as a wonderful reminder of your love and commitment.

68. Make a proposal crossword puzzle. This is a great challenge for crossword puzzle lover. Make a custom crossword puzzle with your proposal in the clues. When the puzzle is complete, it should be obvious what it is. Use an online puzzle creator or, if you're up for a challenge, make your own crossword puzzle by hand.

69. Make a fishy proposal. If you live near an aquarium, call and ask if they're willing to help you stage your proposal in their biggest tank. A diver carrying a "Will you marry me?" message is bound to get her attention. Have your ring at the ready and drop to one knee as soon as she spots it.

70. Live stream your proposal. A live stream is a great way to involve family and friends who are scattered around the globe. If the woman you love is also away at the moment, you have all the more reasons to start a live stream. If you're already a streamer, you're halfway there. Set up a stream on one of the many broadcasting services online, and have everyone tune in at the same time. When your loved ones are all there, ask her to watch your stream and make sure the camera can see you get down on one knee.

71. Take her to the Taj Mahal. Any of the wonders of the world make for a great proposal location, but the Taj Mahal especially so. Built by Emperor Shah Jahan to house the tomb of his wife, it's a testament to love that lasts beyond earthly bounds.

72. Propose with a song at karaoke. There is any number of songs that make for a great proposal tune. You can change the lyrics to her favorite song a little or go with Train's tailor-made folk-rock hit Marry Me.

73. Propose under the mistletoe. The holiday season brings out the love in all of us. Ask her for a kiss under the mistletoe and surprise her with the ring. It makes for a great photo opportunity that your

family can help with.

74. Deliver your proposal with a pizza. Plan this for the next time you have a pizza night together, and when you put in the order, ask them to write your proposal message in the box. Have her open the pizza when it arrives and wait behind her with the ring when she does.
75. Make a proposal on the green. If you're both into golf, this works great on a real course, but it's just as effective with mini-golf. When you sink your put, pretend you found something in the hole and struggle with it until she comes over. You'll already be on one knee, and all you have to do then is show her what you found — her engagement ring.
76. Propose 30,000 feet in the air. You'll have to be very discreet for this one on your next flight together. Talk to the airline staff at the airport about announcing your proposal on the intercom of the plane. They'll let you know if they can do it during the flight or after you land. Be sure to have the ring prepared and be ready for applause.
77. Propose at a parade. If you live in or near a small town, you're no stranger to parades. Go to the town's administrative office and find out if you can have someone in the parade help you propose. They might even get the marching band to play a song just for you.
78. Propose during a meteor shower. If you've never witnessed a meteor shower, you're missing out. It's a stunning display of cosmic majesty and a terrific opportunity to propose. Find out when the next meteor shower is going to happen nearby and arrange a trip to a secluded location. While she's marveling at the spectacle going on above, surprise her with the ring.
79. Let a snowman be your wingman. On a snowy day, build a snowman facing away from your home and put a sign in his hands with your proposal. Ask her to inspect your work when you finish and get ready for the tears of joy.
80. Propose at the theater. The play "I Love You, You're Perfect, Now Change" has become known for staging proposals. If there's a pro-

duction near you, get tickets for a night out and contact the stage manager well in advance. The management will walk you through the process to get you up on stage at the right time and let you declare your everlasting love.

81. Record a proposal podcast. If she loves podcasts, this is bound to be her favorite podcast of all time. Recording a podcast is easy and you don't even need to publish it. Just sneak it into her playlist and wait for her to hear it.

82. Propose with the help of her favorite author. Get a copy of her favorite book, take it to a book signing, and ask for a special dedication. If the author won't be coming to your area anytime soon, try emailing them and sending the copy. Make sure you have the perfect message; don't expect the author to come up with something for you. When you give her the book, ask her to read the dedication.

83. Propose at the end of a race. If you're runners or adventure racers, consider proposing at the finish line of a race. The natural rush of endorphins will set the perfect mood for an unforgettable proposal.

84. Propose on a billboard. Renting a billboard shouldn't be too much trouble. Make sure you come up with a short and sweet message that's obviously meant for her. You can pick any billboard, as long as you can come up with an excuse to get her to see it.

85. Plant a fake book at the library. This might cause her to get suspicious if you don't play it right. Make a fake book where you put the ring and your proposal and plant it in the correct place on the shelf at the library. Insist that you need that particular book and you can't get it any other way. When she helps you find the book, let her open it and see what's inside.

86. Propose during a traffic stop. You'll need a friend in the police force for this proposal. Talk to your friend beforehand to see if he's OK with helping you. Have him pull her over and while he's talking to her, sneak up on her driver's side door with the ring in hand.

HOW TO PROPOSE

87. Prepare breakfast in bed. This is a very simple and effective proposal. Everyone loves breakfast in bed, but the special touch will be a ring on the tray when you bring it to her.
88. Lead her with a trail of petals. You can do this in your home or at a venue that's willing to help you. Create a trail of petals leading to a dinner table or to you and have her come to the location. When she reaches the end of the trail, she will probably figure out what's happening, so all you have to do is show her the ring and ask her to be your wife.
89. Get your proposal on a theater marquee. You'll probably have more luck with a smaller theater than a big chain. Talk to the theater manager to place a special marquee with your proposal. Take a walk together and direct her attention to the marquee. Your photographer can wait by the theater and capture the moment.
90. Propose on a climb. Wall climbing can be a fun activity even if you don't have much experience. Schedule a couples' class at a climbing gym and tell the instructors that you want to propose. They can help you do everything safely. You can have them put your proposal message at the top of a climb or just wait for her with the ring when she comes down.
91. Propose in the future. Have her join you in putting together a time capsule that you're planning to bury in your back yard and have fun looking for interesting things to put in it. The last thing should be a card with the date and the message "The day we got engaged."
92. Create a restaurant at home. Learn to cook her favorite ethnic dish and create a restaurant atmosphere in your home. Have a friend meet her at the door as the restaurant's "host" and another that will be your waiter for the evening. When she's thoroughly speechless, show her the ring.
93. Proposal at a casting call. Enlist the aid of your local film school to fake a casting call for the two of you to star in a student film. Tell

her you entered the casting call as a joke, but they're looking for a man and a woman. The casting call will be for a scene in which the man proposes to the woman. Of course, you won't be acting.

94. Take her to the place you first met. This doesn't have to be very complicated, but you can make it as fancy as you like. Set up the place where you first met and find an excuse to go there together. If it's outdoors, set it up to look like your living room and put up a lot of pictures of you together. Remembering the place will be enough, but the extra effort will really pay off.
95. Propose on a camping trip. Sharing a tent can be a very romantic experience. Tie the ring to the tent's zipper while she sleeps and let her discover it when she wakes up. If you can make a trip to a mountain, the scenery will make a big difference.
96. Propose on a cruise. Cruise proposals may sound a bit overplayed, but they're still effective. Propose on your first day at sea to have the rest of the cruise as a celebration. Proposals on cruise ships are common and the crew will help you pick the right place and time.
97. Write your proposal on the wall. If you're planning on repainting a wall in your home, get a head start by writing your proposal on it. To really elevate this proposal, paint it on the wall of a new home for the two of you.
98. Propose under the northern lights. This will take more than a little planning, but it has one of the biggest payoffs. Plan a trip to a place where the aurora can be seen with some regularity. Make a nightly vigil and use nature's most beautiful spectacle to serve as the setting for your proposal.
99. Recreate your favorite proposal. Think of her (or your) favorite proposal from a movie, TV show, or history and recreate it as faithfully as possible. Be as careful as you can about the details. The more elaborate you make it, the better the memory.

HOW TO PROPOSE

OUR 10 FAVORITE PROPOSALS OF ALL TIME

There are proposals, and then there are proposals. The marriage proposal holds a special place in our culture's heart. Proposing is a magical occasion not just for the couple, but also for everyone else involved in their lives. Proposals are a symbol of hope — the hope that there's someone out there for everyone and that one day it could happen to us. A marriage proposal is one of the best ways to reach the climax of a beautiful love affair and let the audience know that everything is going to be alright. Today it's seen in countless romantic movies, books, and TV shows. However, proposing isn't a new tradition by any means. In fact, the origin of the marriage proposal ceremony is thought to originate from the Talmud, one of the principal texts in Jewish law. With so much history and tradition and pop culture to draw from, it's difficult to decide what exactly it is that makes one stand out from the rest. Nevertheless, not all proposals are created equal. A complete list of all the proposals that have gone above and beyond expectations would fill a library, so here is an abbreviated list of ten famous proposals that were total show-stoppers.

1. Edward Rochester's proposal to Jane Eyre. Charlotte Brontë's magnum opus about the governess of Thornfield Hall sees the titular character receive not one but two proposals. They're both romantic in their own way, but the one that stands out is the first for being so unexpected. When Mr. Rochester proposes to Jane, he doesn't make it a single grand gesture but teases her and prolongs the conversation to get at her true feelings. When her feelings are finally exposed, he asks her to come to sit by him and she refuses. Then he delivers that famous line, "But, Jane, I summon you as my wife: it is you only I intend to marry."
2. Andrew Henning's proposal in *Sweet Home Alabama*. When it

comes to grand gestures, it doesn't get much grander than this. In the movie *Sweet Home Alabama*, Andrew Henning proposes to his girlfriend Melanie in the most spectacular way. He leads her to a dark room, and when she's completely bewildered, the lights come on. They are revealed to be in a jewelry showroom, and they have it all to themselves. Andrew tells Melanie to pick out any ring she wants as her engagement ring. Talk about over the top!

3. Jim's proposal to Pam in *The Office*. When everyone's favorite TV couple finally got engaged, it came as no surprise. After a will-they-won't-they lasting several seasons of the show, the moment finally arrives after a ruined first attempt. Tired of waiting for the perfect moment, Jim asks Pam to meet him for lunch halfway between Scranton and New York. He proposes as soon as they see each other. The symbolism of meeting someone halfway is the ideal way to understand marriage.

4. Benedick's proposal to Beatrice in *Much Ado About Nothing*. No one could write a love story like The Bard. In *Much Ado About Nothing*, Shakespeare tells the tale of two star-crossed lovers, but it's the minor story of Benedick and Beatrice that truly shines. From the very start, Benedick is presented as a clever wordsmith who swears to never marry. Meeting his match in Beatrice, they have frequent squabbles throughout the play. Their quick-witted jabs continue until the very end when Benedick finally exclaims: "Peace! I will stop your mouth." And he does — by kissing her.

5. Robbie's proposal to Julia in *The Wedding Singer*. Robbie is fed up with love and relationships before he realizes that Julia is the girl for him. A wedding singer by trade, he chooses to serenade Julia in his proposal. This happens after he finds out that they happen to be on the same airplane. Through a comical twist of fate, he enlists the help of Billy Idol to deal with her current fiancé. It's a romantic comedy and meant to be extravagant to the point of hilarity. Julia

and Robbie's story reminds us that we all deserve happiness, but sometimes a little help from our friends goes a long way.
6. Mr. Darcy's second proposal in *Pride and Prejudice*. Mr. Darcy initially demeans Elizabeth, seeing her as below his station. However, he soon finds himself enthralled by her against his better judgment. When he decides to propose, his arrogance and hypocrisy repels her. Her refusal sparks in him a long episode of soul searching and he returns months later with renewed hope. Having reconsidered his stance, he approaches her with humility and honesty. This time she accepts and another great love story has a happy ending.
7. Johnny Cash's proposal to June Carter. This iconic country music couple had many ups and downs. After many failed attempts at proposing, the Man in Black picked his moment at a show in Ontario where they were performing together. He had told the band what he would do asked her to marry him immediately after finishing a duet. June demurred and asked the band to keep playing, but they wouldn't budge. After some insistence, she finally said yes and the rest is history.
8. Chandler's proposal to Monica in *Friends*. It took six seasons of one of the most successful sitcoms of all time for this proposal to finally happen. Technically, it's Monica who proposes to Chandler, but she can't finish her speech after getting choked up. Chandler steps in to save the day with his famous line: "You make me happier than I ever thought I could be, and if you let me, I will spend the rest of my life trying to make you feel the same way." Sometimes, a candlelit apartment and true love are the only things you need.
9. Jamie's proposal to Aurélia in *Love Actually*. The movie *Love Actually* is a complex exploration of the various ways we fall in love — but the main love story is between Jamie and his housekeeper Aurélia. She only speaks Portuguese and he only speaks English, but love conquers the language barrier. After returning to England

from France, Jamie learns Portuguese so he can propose. When he delivers his awkward speech in Portuguese, we learn that Aurélia has also been learning English to do the same.
10. Charles' proposal to Emma in Madame Bovary. Flaubert's Charles Bovary is a tragic character. After struggling through medical school, he marries a woman whom he doesn't love and she dies soon after. He soon meets a farmer's daughter, and instead of proposing to Emma directly, he plans to ask her father and struggles to say the words. Realizing what's going on, Emma's father saves him and tells Charles to wait outside the house. He tells Charles he will open the shutters of the house if his daughter agrees. Charles counts the minutes — nineteen to be exact — before the shutter swings open.

An honorable mention goes to the movie Jerry Maguire. Jerry, played by Tom Cruise, doesn't exactly propose. He delivers a speech to his wife to try to win her back after a separation. The entire movie he plays an underdog and when he finally succeeds, he realizes how pointless it all was because he lost her in the process. His speech has all the hallmarks of a proposal, and when he reaches the emotional climax, his wife stops him with a line that still echoes in our hearts — "You had me at hello."

Literary characters often have to struggle and propose several times before it pays off. Hopefully, you won't have to do that. Another thing to keep in mind is that a proposal — especially a complicated one — can go wrong in a lot of ways. Always have a backup plan if things don't go as expected.

Now that you've got an arsenal of proposal ideas, it's time to work on the proposal speech.

WHAT TO SAY DURING THE PROPOSAL

The most important thing to remember is to let your proposal speech come from your heart. It's better to have a short and earnest speech than something extravagant and contrived. There's no need for you to have a written speech. After all, you're just putting your feelings into words. Don't worry if you stumble and forget a few key points.

Don't try to be anything but who you truly are. She already loves you, so make sure your true self comes through in the speech. There are going to be all sorts of emotions flying around and it's OK to let yourself get emotional. If you get choked up, you won't be showing weakness but your overwhelming love.

Start the speech with a line or two about how you felt when you first met. This can be an amusing story, but don't go into too much detail. Just tell her how she won you over. That will make a perfect segue to tell her when you decided to marry her. You don't want to be too specific, rather you want her to know what tipped you off that you were meant to be.

Don't make it sound like you're just telling her what you think she wants to hear. Speak a bit about what she has done to make you a better person. Talk about all the positive changes in your life that wouldn't have been possible without her.

Then finish with some shared goals and values. The two of you are about to embark on a journey through life together, so it would be good to point out the ways in which you can help each other. Family, work ethic, and security are just some of the things that you'll be working on together. Most importantly, briefly describe the kind of future you envision for the two of you.

You want to end with the question, but not before you make a promise. Make her feel safe for choosing you by promising to choose her every day for the rest of your life.

CHAPTER 5
CARING FOR YOUR ENGAGEMENT RING

Nobody likes to think about losing something precious to them, but the reality of life is that things get damaged or lost regularly. In the case of engagement rings, the tears of joy that came from first seeing it can easily turn into tears of pain if it goes missing — and they go missing more often than you might think.

Caring for your engagement ring doesn't take too much effort. Rings are mostly designed to be unobtrusive and functional, so a modicum of attention will go a long way. Getting into the habit of taking some common-sense precautions is all it takes. In a perfect world, your ring should last long enough to get passed down through generations, so it's worth the effort that it takes to preserve it.

Throughout its lifespan, your ring will probably suffer minor to moderate harm, which is nothing to worry about. Any skilled jeweler will be able to repair or modify your engagement ring within reason. However, the one thing that no one can repair is the loss of a ring; replacing it won't be easy, but a comprehensive insurance plan can certainly help.

There's a whole different host of considerations when it comes to insuring a ring, so that's the best place to start discussing ring care.

HOW TO INSURE YOUR RING

Some people feel there's something hypocritical about replacing an engagement ring. After all, you can't replace your ring any more than you can replace your fiancée, right?

Surely, there's something sacred about that ring that makes it more than just another piece of jewelry. It's not just any ring; it's the ring that symbolizes your love and affection, but these semantic details tend to fall away very quickly when faced with the potential loss of thousands of dollars of equity.

While the sadness and frustration of losing your engagement ring won't be completely mitigated by replacing it, at least you can recover some of the investment. Engagement rings span a broad range of prices from as little as a few hundred dollars to Elizabeth Taylor's famous $8.8 million ring.

If you purchased a relatively affordable ring, the insurance is likely to be just as affordable. If your ring is more lavish, then it makes that much more sense to insure it. As a rule of thumb, insure any jewelry you can't easily replace on your own.

To fully understand how to handle your ring insurance, you should first learn the options that are available. Work your way through this section at your own pace and try to keep some of the terminology in the back of your mind. When it's finally time to purchase your insurance, this will help you negotiate the right kind and price.

Homeowners Insurance

As a renter or homeowner, you are likely to have some degree of personal property insurance that covers jewelry. This would encompass your engagement ring, but it's usually quite limited and very rarely covers the loss of a ring. You'll be protected in the case of things like theft or some natural disasters, but not much else.

This type of insurance is better than nothing but isn't recommended as your only insurance. Policies will vary, but they typically range from $1,000 to $2,000 of coverage for jewelry. A better option is to upgrade your current insurance in the form of a rider — specifically, a type of rider called a floater.

Adding a Rider

A rider adds a provision to an existing insurance policy to cover something that the policy doesn't otherwise extend to. Adding a rider to your insurance policy is common for areas where you're underinsured, and when you acquire something expensive such as an engagement ring, you're likely to be underinsured.

A floater is a kind of insurance policy that covers loss or theft of easily movable property. Floaters usually cover one single item, so if you have several items — and this isn't restricted to jewelry — you will need a floater for each. This type of policy will cover any kind of loss, including mysterious disappearance (an industry term for an unexplained loss). You will have to produce an appraisal to cover your engagement ring with a floater.

Specialized Jewelry Insurance

This last kind of policy is specially designed for jewelry and is often going to be your best choice for a high-end ring. This option won't be available from every insurance provider and you may even want to find one that specializes in jewelry. Items covered by this type of policy will typically be protected from any kind of loss, theft, or damage.

In most cases, you will be able to choose a deductible that works for you, which will help offset the cost of the policy. Specialized policies for jewelry will require an appraisal and should range in cost between 1% and 2% of the value of the ring. Another important benefit is that claims on this policy won't count against your homeowner's insurance.

Before you sign on with any insurance company, you should find out what exactly it is that they are offering. This means finding out what is covered and what isn't under the policy. To that end, you might have to go through some fine print, but you will have an easier time if you speak to an agent and ask the right questions. Here are the things you should learn when choosing jewelry insurance:

- First and foremost, ask about the insurance plans that are available. It's best to start with an overview of the options and then evaluate what fits you best. This will give you information on what the policy covers, but it's just as important — if not more — to ask about what it doesn't cover.
- Learn about any restrictions on where you can replace or repair your ring. Some insurance companies will allow you to pick your jeweler, but others partner with specific ones.
- Ask about what your deductible options are. Customizable deductibles are a sign that the company has reliable underwriters and they help tailor the cost of your policy to your circumstances.
- Insurance premiums are largely dependent on your area of resi-

CARING FOR YOUR ENGAGEMENT RING

dence due to a lot of factors such as theft rates. This could impact your insurance premium if you move, so make sure you're clear about if and how a move affects your premium.
- Where does the coverage stop? If your policy only extends within national borders, you'll be out of luck if the ring is lost on a trip abroad.
- How does the company handle claims? You should be clear about exactly what you'll need to provide if you ever need to replace or repair your ring. Replacement vs. actual cash value will also be covered in this chapter.
- The best way to cover your bases is to ask an open-ended question. For instance, "Is there anything I should have asked that I didn't?" Insurance agents will never lie to you, so as long as you take your time, it should be easy to get insured properly.

The kind of insurance you choose will depend on your specific situation and circumstances, but assuming you're going to purchase a comprehensive policy, you will need a few important documents starting with an appraisal. Having proof of purchase is important, but the appraisal is going to have the largest effect on the price of your policy.

Some insurance companies will require the use of a specific appraisal service, but most specialized insurers will allow you to select the one you want as long as it's certified. Before moving on, you should note that a grading report is not an appraisal.

Grading reports are covered in an earlier chapter and they pertain to the quality of the stone in the ring. The report will be part of the appraisal of the ring, but it doesn't do much for you if you're filing a claim on an unappraised ring. The purpose of the report will be to assist in making an accurate appraisal and you should receive one when you purchase a ring with a substantial diamond.

When getting your ring appraised, you're aiming for an accurate price. Having a ring under-appraised will leave you with less than you need to replace it should a claim be necessary. Conversely, an over-appraised ring will needlessly increase your insurance premium. That's not the only liability — if a piece is incorrectly valued, insurance companies can use this as a reason to avoid settling a claim.

Keep in mind that quality jewelry tends to appreciate in value, so it's a good idea to have it reappraised every five to ten years and adjust your insurance policy accordingly.

Vintage and antique rings will require a special standard of care. If you're trying to appraise one, find a jeweler that specializes in vintage jewelry as there are specific criteria that will greatly impact their value.

The highest contribution to a ring's value is going to come from the stone. The quality of the stone will be part of the appraisal, as will the cut, type of metal, and many other qualities of the ring. Subsequent evaluations after the first one will be less expensive and time-consuming if you can provide the previous appraisal.

Another important but often overlooked part of the insurance process is pictures of the ring. Insurance companies won't insist that you provide these, but you'll be glad you did. The photos will be especially useful in cases where the ring becomes damaged, allowing for proper reimbursement for legitimate repairs that are made.

When you've settled on the right insurance policy, provided all the relevant documentation, and signed the dotted line, you can almost rest easy. The ideal scenario is one in which you never have to use your insurance policy, but you should know what you're entitled to and how to claim it if it ever comes to that.

If you go the homeowner's insurance route (and in some cases with specialized providers), the process is going to be pretty straightforward. In case of loss, you'll make a claim, provide the required proof to settle the claim, and receive a check for the value of the ring. Of course, that's a highly superficial outline and leaves out a lot of things, but it gets to the important issue, which is how much you'll be getting from the insurance.

The insurance policy will state whether you're entitled to the actual cash value of the ring or a replacement cost. The actual cash value will pay out damages to the insured property minus depreciation. Since we established that jewelry sometimes appreciates in value, this isn't an ideal scenario. You could end up getting a much lower settlement than what you're really owed based on the actual cash value.

The alternative is a replacement policy. With this type of policy, you'll get the declared value of the property regardless of value fluctuations. This is a better option for jewelry and much simpler overall. Rather than expect your insurance provider to be sensitive to the antique nature of a ring or other confounding factors, you're well-advised to just select a replacement policy.

If your insurance policy covers damages, you will be reimbursed for repairs resulting from impact damages. However, very rarely will a policy cover wear and tear sustained under normal use conditions.

Finally, you should be aware of what kind of proof of loss you'll need to provide when filing a claim. Most insurance companies that work with jewelry will trust a loss claim if the policy covers it, but some will need added proof. This is best cleared up by speaking with an agent. Make sure you're completely clear as to under what circumstances you need to provide evidence and to what extent.

In case of theft, insurance companies will usually require a police report. Make sure you report theft or robbery of your ring to the authorities as soon as possible as this will impact your claim.

There are a few basic things that aren't covered in-depth here in the service of brevity — such as deductibles and exclusions — but you should have everything you need to make an educated decision. As long as you choose a reputable provider and you ask all the right questions, you'll be able to rest easy.

WHEN TO TAKE OFF YOUR RING

Diamonds are the toughest naturally occurring material on earth, but this doesn't make your ring or your stones indestructible. If you're like most people, the first really expensive piece of jewelry you'll buy is a diamond engagement ring.

Many people choose to wear an engagement ring daily as a token of their commitment to their relationship. There's nothing wrong with this, but an engagement ring deserves special care — both for sentimental reasons and because it's an expensive piece of jewelry.

Diamonds are very resilient, but they're not indestructible. You should also take into account that the diamonds aren't the only part of the ring. In fact, the part that's least likely to get damaged is the stone. It's much more likely that a prong might come loose (thereby dislodging the diamond) or the metal becomes dull or scratched.

There's little point in having a big and beautiful stone if its splendid brilliance is going to be inhibited by grime and dirt. It's important that you keep your ring clean to expose the natural beauty it possesses. Aside from regular cleanings, you should also take your ring off in certain situations.

Try to be pragmatic about when and where a ring is in peril. There's no practical way to cover every situation where a ring should be removed (such as skydiving or rock climbing), but there are reasonably common activities and places when taking off your ring is a good idea.

Consider that you'll be wearing your ring most of the time, most days, for the rest of your life. This is a long time, and much like a stalagmite, the damage to an engagement ring will compound over time. Take the following sections as a guide to when a ring should be put away, but rely on common sense in general.

At the Beach

At this point it's a cliché to hear someone go on about how they lost their ring at the beach. Losing rings on the beach is so common that there are actually groups of volunteer ring finders that can be contacted over the internet who specialize in finding lost engagement rings. The brunt of the rings they find are lost at beaches all around the world.

There's nothing magical about beaches that attracts rings, it's simply a combination of the relaxed atmosphere, sand getting lodged in between a finger and the ring, and oily sunscreen providing lubrication for jewelry to slide off undetected.

Sunscreen, in particular, is a bugbear for engagement rings. It will make a stone cloudy and dull instantly and it's difficult to clean off. It's prudent to take your ring off when heading for the beach; if you're about to set off on vacation, consider leaving your ring behind in a secure location just to be on the safe side. Nothing hides a ring quite like sand.

Going Swimming

The beach isn't the only place you'll be going for a swim. In general, water will make it easier for a ring to slide off a finger, but there are other reasons why it's smart to remove it while swimming. Water (cold water in particular) will cause blood vessels to constrict, reducing the size of fingers and helping a ring to come loose.

On top of that, the harsh chemicals of a pool or saltwater of the ocean can have serious detrimental effects on the stones and metal of the ring. Any pool is likely to be treated with a variety of harsh chemicals, all of which will dampen the luster and brilliance of an engagement ring over time.

Some metals are exceptionally susceptible to chemicals. Rhodium, for instance, will turn yellow when exposed to chlorine. To prevent this, make sure any jewelry is taken off before entering the water. If at all possible, plan ahead and leave it at home before you go swimming.

When Cooking

A ring around a finger creates many little nooks and crannies in which bacteria can find a home. When handling any kind of raw meat or other perishables, it's a good idea to remove your ring. Additionally, you'll probably be doing a lot of hand-washing, which can put your ring at risk of falling down the drain.

All that washing will also expose rings to products that may degrade the appearance of the metal. Finally, along the same lines, grease will restrict the light that reaches a ring. If a ring gets greasy, it will lose some of its sparkle.

When Exercising

This one is more or less obvious but worth mentioning. Whether you like to work out at a gym or outdoors, you're likely to be using your hands quite a bit. On the one hand, all that gripping and grasping heavy weights will a) deform or otherwise damage the ring's shank and b) cause discomfort by digging into the finger.

It is probably OK to keep a ring on for a quick cardio session, especially indoors. However, any kind of extreme or contact sports puts the ring in jeopardy.

CARING FOR YOUR ENGAGEMENT RING

During Pregnancies

Pregnancy is a time of significant physical change for women. It's very likely that fluctuations in water retention and weight will cause ring sizes to vary. Nearing the end of a pregnancy in particular causes a ring size to change quite drastically.

The best way to deal with this is to stop wearing the ring when it starts to feel tight. Some women want to continue wearing a ring throughout their pregnancy, and in that case, an inexpensive proxy that is larger can be used. No jewelry should be worn at hospitals for a variety of reasons, so definitely leave the ring behind during the delivery.

Engaging in Manual Labor

Gardening, auto repair, and even house cleaning are good examples of times when your ring should come off. Rings should be removed in any situation that requires gloves. On top of the potential damage that the ring could sustain from chemicals or impacts, getting a ring caught in moving machinery is extremely dangerous.

In 2015, late-night talk show host Jimmy Fallon shared the gruesome details of getting his ring caught on a counter during a fall which led to hours of surgery and a ten-day period in an intensive care unit. Of course, that was a freak accident and not very common, but it should make people rethink putting themselves in situations where a ring can be dangerous.

Around Cosmetics

Not all cosmetic products will have adverse effects on the ring, but in general, it is best to be conservative about exposing it to things like hairspray and moisturizers. Remember that oil and grease diminish the light that your stone will catch, so don't let lotions build up on it. It shouldn't be too much of a chore to remove the ring while engaging in self-care routines and replacing it once your hands are completely dry.

On the Wedding Day

This is more of a personal choice. Ultimately, only the two of you can decide what kind of wedding will make you happy. However, it's worth noting that many people feel that an engagement ring takes the spotlight away from the more modest wedding band.

If it's worn for the wedding, it's a good idea to place it on the third finger of the left hand to make room for the wedding band. Additionally, it's traditional to take pictures of the couple's ring-clad hands, and some people feel that it's much more impactful if these pictures feature only the wedding bands. But, once again, there are no traditional rules about wearing engagement rings at weddings. It's just something to keep in mind.

It bears repeating that this is a practical guide that doesn't cover every potential situation which could jeopardize an engagement ring. Nor should this guide be taken to be some sort of code that needs to be followed to the letter. You shouldn't feel as though an engagement ring needs so much pampering that it's not even worth wearing.

Recently, it has become a trend among very active people to wear placeholder rings instead of their engagement rings and wedding

CARING FOR YOUR ENGAGEMENT RING

bands. Professional athletes, in particular, find this to be a very convenient way to maintain their emotional connection with their spouse without making it an inconvenience to their craft. Silicone rings are a popular choice for this purpose.

Companies that specialize in silicone rings have very attractive options that can fit most people's styles. Silicone is very malleable, and these rings will not sustain injury except in the most extreme cases. The sheer strength of these rings is also much lower than metal ones, so they'll tear apart well before there's any danger of causing harm.

A ring's place is on a finger, and any time it's taken off, there's a chance it could be lost or misplaced. To avoid mishaps, it's a good idea to have designated locations to keep a ring when it's not being worn. A jewelry box is an obvious choice, but it can become a chore to make frequent trips to it.

Rather than have just one location, set up a few around the areas where the ring is likely to come off, such as the kitchen, garage, or home gym. Even something as simple as a small saucer can be perfectly suitable as a ring rest.

An ounce of prevention is worth a pound of cure when deciding whether or not to take off an engagement ring. Some are quite delicate and will require extraordinary care — to the point that it's best to not wear them at all save for special occasions.

CLEANING THE RING

Seeing a ring regain its natural sparkle after it's been cleaned is almost magical. Most rings, and especially engagement rings, are meant to draw the eye, and that's a tall order if the metal is dull or the stone cloudy. If a ring is worn with any kind of regularity (most days of the week), it will require cleaning to keep it looking beautiful.

There are no real rules about when a ring should be cleaned, but a simple examination is a good way to determine if it needs some attention. Otherwise, a cleaning schedule of every few weeks or once a month works for many people.

Cleaning engagement rings is not much different from cleaning any piece of jewelry, but there are some special considerations that should be taken into account. Broadly speaking, the two options are to take the ring to a jeweler to get it professionally cleaned or to clean it at home. Whether it will be taken to a jeweler at some point shouldn't preclude owners from regularly cleaning their ring at home as well.

For a home cleaning, all you need is some warm water and dishwashing liquid (shampoo also works). Make sure the cleaning product you choose isn't moisturizing as these tend to leave a film behind that is counterproductive to the cleaning. It's also good to have a soft bristle toothbrush to dislodge any accumulated grime on the ring.

Here is a step-by-step walkthrough of the cleaning process:

1. Fill a small bowl with warm water and add dishwashing liquid to it. You won't need very much, just enough to form a light lather.
2. Place the ring in the bowl and let it sit for about five to ten minutes. The detergent action of the soap will dissolve any oils and dislodge dirt and grime. There's no benefit to soaking the ring for longer than that, and you certainly shouldn't soak it overnight.
3. Retrieve the ring and examine it. In many cases, it won't require any extra work, but in case it's still got some stubborn dirt or smudges, use the soft bristle toothbrush to scrub around the stone and in any hard-to-reach places, always employing a light touch. Pavé settings are especially susceptible to grime buildup in the tiny prongs and crenelations that hold all the diamonds in place.
4. Rinse the ring in cold water and pat it dry with a soft cotton cloth. Don't use paper towels as these can have traces of abrasive ma-

terials in the fibers which can scratch the ring. Allow the ring to air-dry completely before putting it back on.

This procedure is completely safe and will never harm your diamond ring if followed properly even if a ring is cleaned very frequently.

The fewer chemicals you use to clean jewelry, the longer it will last. Dishwashing liquid is very mild and thus suitable for the task, but anything more aggressive is bound to cause problems with extended use. Particularly, any kind of spirits or traditional solvents such as acetone, paint thinner, or vinegar shouldn't be used. They'll definitely get the job done, but they're far too caustic for use on precious metals. Some experts advocate using a quick vinegar bath to bring out the shine after a ring has been cleaned, but the difference this makes is really not worth it.

Jewelry cleaning products should also be avoided for two reasons. First, they can be pretty expensive, and they won't do a much better job of cleaning the ring than regular soap and water. The other reason is that some of these cleaning solutions aren't formulated very well, and it's not worth finding that out the hard way.

Ultrasonic cleaners are quite popular for jewelry and professionals use them regularly, but they're not recommended for engagement rings. To understand why, you should have a basic idea of how they work. Ultrasonic cleaners use sound waves to shake up a liquid (typically water), and when something is placed in that liquid, any small particles get slowly shaken out of it.

They work very well, but all that shaking can loosen stones from their setting with extended use. Again, pavé settings should especially be kept out of ultrasonic cleaners due to their delicate nature. Ultrasonic cleaning should be reserved for jewelry without settings, in which case it's not only safe, but it works very well.

Although it's typical for engagement rings to use diamonds, other stones are common as well. Diamonds are very tough, as was pointed out earlier in this chapter, and can take quite a bit of punishment. Other stones, however, tend to be more fragile and susceptible to both scratches and chips. To stay on the safe side, never use hot water to clean your rings and certainly steer clear from any abrasives — toothpaste, baking soda, and polishing compounds are completely out of the question.

Now, if your ring has diamonds and only diamonds, a good way to clean it is to soak it in window cleaner. Window cleaner is a weak ammonia solution and works like a charm for cleaning jewelry. It's a matter of coating the ring with window cleaner and using a soft bristle brush to lightly scrub it all around. Then, rinse it in cold water and allow it to dry. It's critical that you don't use this method for any other stones.

The other method to keep rings looking as sparkly as the day you bought them is to have them professionally cleaned. Most jewelers will offer this service, and if you have a warranty, cleanings are usually included free of charge. Taking your ring in for a cleaning is also a great chance for the jeweler to inspect the setting and make sure that there are no loose stones and any other potential problems in the making. This type of cleaning and checkup should be done about once or twice a year. Even though it may seem logical to use products that are designed to clean jewelry, you're better off avoiding them at home. Ultrasonic cleaners can loosen the settings and cleaning solutions may not be safe on all metals. When in doubt, have your ring professionally cleaned to eliminate any guesswork. Don't allow too much time to pass between cleanings; the more dirt and grime that is allowed to build up, the more difficult it will be to clean, thereby increasing the risk of damage to the ring.

CARING FOR YOUR ENGAGEMENT RING

HOW TO FIX THE RING IF SOMETHING BREAKS

While true love may be eternal, material possessions fall well short of that. The simple fact is that regardless of how careful you are with your ring, it's going to get damaged given enough time. There's no way to guarantee the safety of your ring, but that shouldn't seem like a grim prognosis. Engagement rings can be repaired, and minor repairs won't be expensive or compromise the integrity of the ring.

Whatever the case may be, you should only allow trained jewelers to work on your ring. There are certain guidelines that need to be followed to ensure no further damage is done that only special training will teach. You should never try to perform any repairs on your own; even if the damage is something that seems remarkably simple, such as a slightly bent shank, it will cost you nothing to get it examined and receive advice on the best course of action.

Should it become necessary to take your ring to a jeweler for repairs, lay down some groundwork before you go. Unless you're going to the same jeweler who sold you the ring, you should give them as much information as possible. This includes the type of metal used, any special instructions you have for repairs, and anything you don't want to be changed. If you have lab certifications and/or grading reports, provide these as well and make sure to document the state in which you hand over the ring.

If and when you do take a ring in for repairs, they will fall into one or more of three broad categories: repairs to the stone, setting, or band/shank. In truth, there is one more type of repair which most people don't think of as such — and that's resizing. Resizing will be addressed in a separate section, so for now, let's start with damages to the stone and the relevant repairs.

As tough as diamonds are, they often suffer minor chips and abrasions after prolonged wear; and even slight damage to a diamond or other gemstone will greatly impact its brilliance. Those two types of damage — chips and abrasions — are by far the most common when it comes to stones, and they are repaired in one of two ways: either you'll get the stone restored or replaced.

In the third type of stone-related damage, some people may want an occlusion removed. This is not recommended as the stone will need to be completely redesigned, but if it will very significantly increase the clarity, it may be worth it.

Most of the information that follows is going to be referring to a primary stone that is damaged.

If accents in the setting are lost or chipped, they can be replaced easily and for relatively low cost. Having said that, the situation is a little different when dealing with a much more valuable diamond. If you've got the wherewithal to do so, it may be your best option to replace a chipped or damaged stone, but rarely will it be the only option.

A chipped diamond should be dealt with as soon as circumstances allow. Once a stone is chipped, its structural integrity is compromised and it becomes susceptible to further cracks and cleavage. Whatever you choose to do, a chipped stone shouldn't be worn and you shouldn't delay repairing it.

If the goal is to keep the ring looking as identical as possible, then replacing the stone is the way to go. If the chipped stone is not too badly injured, it may help offset the cost of a new one, but keep in mind that a diamond's value plummets with flaws. Not every jeweler will be willing to make this type of exchange, but most are. On the other hand, if it's not crucial that the ring keeps its original appearance and if the stone is particularly valuable, re-cutting may be a better option.

Re-cutting a stone is not usually a complicated process and essentially entails reducing the size of the diamond until the chip is removed. Reducing the carat weight is going to also directly reduce the value of a stone. That reduction won't necessarily be catastrophic; depending on the size of the chip, it may only need to be very minimally altered.

Re-cutting should generally be reserved for stones that have high real-world value or are otherwise meaningful for you. Although it's very common, it still requires a skilled hand and doesn't come cheap. You should think of 0.30 carats as a rough break-point where it becomes a better idea to replace than recut a stone.

Also, take into consideration how bad the damage is when having it examined. A jeweler will usually be able to tell you roughly how much of the diamond will need to go. The value you would lose may be better invested in purchasing a new stone. This reduces the whole matter to a cold calculation, but ultimately, only the two of you can decide whether you want to recut or replace a stone.

In the case of scratches, minor nicks, and other small surface damage, the diamond can simply be polished. Polishing a diamond removes practically no weight. It can be done fairly quickly and can make a big difference in a diamond's overall appearance. Repairs to the setting can be much more diverse. The most common cause of repairs on a ring is from damage to the setting, and the most common point of damage to the setting is the prongs. Prongs are quite delicate and are prone to bending and warping much more than, say, a bezel setting. In fact, prongs may suffer damage that is not readily noticeable, which is why it's a good idea to regularly have your ring examined and cleaned at a jeweler. You might also find it useful to use a magnifying glass to examine the prongs periodically for any shifts or bends.

For minor damage, such as a prong that gets bent, it's often possible to position the prongs and secure the stone back in place. If prongs break or become worn, it will be necessary to replace them. If prongs are being replaced, it's a good idea to upgrade them to a sturdier metal or thicker prongs. Antique and vintage rings, in particular, can have vulnerable and intricate settings, so they should be afforded extra care.

As with any other damage to your ring, if a prong comes loose, it creates a domino effect. The other prongs are likely to follow, so stop wearing a ring with damaged prongs until it is repaired.

Another fairly common occurrence is the accent stones getting lost or damaged. This is frequently — but not always — the result of damage to the setting. It is difficult to adequately secure micro diamonds, so losing them isn't a sign of bad craftsmanship and replacing them is usually not very expensive.

Finally, a ring's band can sustain damage from various sources, especially if worn frequently. Minor scratches to the metal of the band are extremely common and affect the overall appearance of the ring. These scratches don't usually require repair, but they can easily be re-polished by any jeweler. However, deeper dents or serious discoloration may require the ring to be recoated. White gold is particularly susceptible to this type of damage and will need to be recoated periodically with rhodium.

Now, if a shank becomes warped, bent, or even cracked, it's a more serious issue. Thin shanks are especially vulnerable, but even a thick shank won't withstand a strong blow without buckling. Most damage to the band can be repaired, but there are limits to any repairs. If the damage is too great, a new ring may need to be considered. Whether that be a replica of the ring or a completely new style is up to you, but you can certainly retain and reuse any stones in the current ring.

Regardless of what repairs are done, make sure you examine the entire ring thoroughly before taking it back. The jeweler that worked on the ring should be able to justify everything that was done, and if you're not satisfied with the work, speak up. Don't leave with a ring that doesn't look the way you want it to.

Remember that some metals and stones are softer than others as some people are more active than others. If you're concerned about not being able to safeguard a ring appropriately, a platinum band with diamonds in a bezel setting is the best choice. That combination provides the safest set of characteristics for an engagement ring. If you do go this route, make sure you're confident about the ring size you need because platinum is challenging to resize.

RESIZING YOUR RING

Just about any ring can be resized to some extent — either sized up to fit a larger finger or sized down to fit a smaller one. A variety of factors affect how well rings sit on a finger, from knuckle size to the width of the band. Additionally, finger sizes change under certain circumstances, so it's a good idea to really consider if resizing is necessary.

Most commonly, engagement rings need to be resized when purchased. Even if you're being careful, it's not unusual to get a ring that is the wrong size for your girlfriend. This is a clear-cut situation in which a ring should be resized. For this reason, some jewelers will offer a complimentary resizing with your ring purchase.

Before resizing a ring, consider the long-term implications. If there are health complications affecting the finger size of the wearer, it may be a better idea to stop wearing the ring temporarily. Weight fluctuations and water retention, especially during pregnancies, are common causes of changing finger sizes. It doesn't make a lot of sense to subject the ring to a resizing only to have it resized again soon.

Seasonal conditions are another frequent cause of physiological change. Some people experience a shrinking of extremities during the winter and in those cases, rings tend to become loose temporarily. It's not recommended to resize a ring for something like that. Instead, consider a ring resizing band to reduce the ring size until you don't need it anymore. These resizing bands are available from retailers in many sizes and material options.

If it ultimately makes sense to resize an engagement ring, the next thing you should worry about is if a ring can be resized at all. While most engagement rings can be resized, some settings make it extremely difficult or even impossible to resize. Silver and gold don't usually present much of a problem, but platinum is more challenging and will require a skilled jeweler.

Channel settings that extend around the entire shank are notoriously difficult to resize to the extent that many jewelers won't resize them for fear of irreparably damaging the ring. In some cases, delicate stones will have to be removed from the band before it is resized, thus adding to the price. Finally, rose gold comes in many tones so it's sometimes difficult to match the exact same color of a ring if material needs to be added. These are just some things to keep in mind when choosing a ring if it's likely to need resizing.

In general, very wide or intricate bands present a problem for resizing. Ask your jeweler if an engagement ring can be resized before committing to it. If it can't be resized, don't buy it blindly — have your girlfriend try the ring on first. This will ruin the surprise, but it will save you from having to choose another ring.

If your engagement ring is a simple band with a simple setting, it can be resized quickly and without any issues, but you should still choose the right person for the job. It is not advisable to take your ring to a chain store because they don't tend to have a jeweler on the premises that does resizing. Instead, the ring is often sent to a headquarters where it is resized. While you can get decent results this way, it's better to opt for a more personal approach if it's available.

Try to speak to the person who will be doing the resizing, explain to them why it needs to be resized, and provide any specific instructions you have. If you can make an impression and convey how much the ring means to you, they're likely to give it extra care. Also, they can

CARING FOR YOUR ENGAGEMENT RING

explain to you what the resizing options are and what they think is the best option for your engagement ring.

As a matter of fact, you should have a basic understanding of the methods used to resize rings. If it needs to be smaller, the most common procedure is to remove a piece of metal from the ring (called a cutout) and then compress the band and solder it at the new size. If this is the method that will be used, don't be afraid to ask for your cutout since you can use it in the future if the ring needs to be sized up. The cutout method isn't the only way to reduce a ring size. Some less-permanent options include sizing beads (or "shots"), a spring insert, or a sizing bar. These are good options if there's an extended period in which a ring will fit loosely but is likely to go back to a snug fit eventually. Several months of cold weather is a good example of this type of situation. Shots are actually quite common and simply involve soldering two small beads to the inside of the ring. They're noticeable by the wearer initially but become unnoticeable within a day or two.

There is also an uncommon solution for people with very large knuckles which involves modifying the band entirely to be more like a bracelet or bangle. This complicated sizing technique is expensive and not performed by many jewelers, but if you have a very valuable ring that you want to keep and wear for years to come, it may be worth it.

Now, making a ring bigger is a little more limiting. There are two practical options — stretching the ring or adding metal to the band. Stretching is where the ring is placed on a mandrel or ring stretching tool and pressure is slowly applied to enlarge it. This is sometimes the only option to enlarge an intricate ring, but there are associated risks so some jewelers will avoid it.

By stretching the ring, it becomes thinner and thereby more susceptible to ends or breaks in the future. Additionally, the ring's appearance can be slightly altered by the warping. In any case, this option shouldn't be used if a ring needs to be more than one size larger. The benefit of stretching the ring is that it's much cheaper and faster than the alternative.

The other option, adding metal, is more expensive but safer for most significant resizing. For this method, a jeweler will sever the ring at the shank and carefully expand the diameter to the correct size. Then, a piece of metal matching the ring is inserted into the remaining cavity and soldered into place. Once it's ground and polished, it will be unnoticeable and the ring should look the same except for being larger.

It's important that you find a trustworthy jeweler that has a proven track record for resizing rings. Every ring is to some extent unique, and many things can go wrong when resizing them — for example, prongs can become warped, gems can come loose, and engravings may become damaged. Consult several jewelers and rely on word-of-mouth recommendations before you choose one to resize your ring.

This is especially important for rings that are challenging to resize. If you can use a locally-owned jewelry store, that will probably be your best bet. Local jewelers will usually give you an honest assessment, and if they can't resize your ring, they can recommend someone who can.

When your ring is resized, make sure to go over it carefully and check for any noticeable changes. If you properly recorded the state of the ring when you handed it over for resizing, these should be easy to spot and inquire about.

- If a ring is cut when it's being resized, this can weaken the shank where the cut was made. Gently press the band of the ring and try to notice any buckling or warping when you do. If the spot where it was cut is perceptible, it is poorly done.
- Examine the band carefully for any narrow or wide spots. If metal was added, sometimes the metal is not carefully shaped around the existing band. If you notice any variations, point them out to the jeweler before you accept the ring.
- Test all the stones with a toothpick to see if any are loose. Prongs

CARING FOR YOUR ENGAGEMENT RING

and settings can get damaged during the resizing and it's important to verify their integrity. Any loose stones should be realigned and fastened.
- Make sure the band doesn't have any differently colored sections. If the right metal isn't used, it can cause areas of the band to look off.

In theory, if a ring is resized correctly, it won't affect its structural integrity in a meaningful way. Even so, it is best to resize rings only when absolutely necessary. Every time a ring is resized, there is a small chance that something might go wrong.

If you have any doubts about whether you should resize a ring, consult a trustworthy jeweler. You won't be charged anything for an assessment, and it's the best way to make the right decision.

CHAPTER 6
WHAT ELSE YOU SHOULD KNOW

At this point, you're most of the way there to knowing everything proposal-related — from the best ways to propose, to choosing diamonds, choosing rings, and even how to navigate jewelry insurance. Now it's time to round off the edges of your education with some details that don't get much attention.

Diamonds are by far the most common stone for engagement rings but certainly not the only one out there. Birthstones are very popular, and cubic zirconia is a great placeholder or substitute when purchasing a ring. As much as we'd like to believe in a love that can't be undone, many people marry more than once. If you're heading into a second engagement, there are a few things you should keep in mind, and they'll be covered here.

Last, but certainly not least, is the uncomfortable issue of getting a ring stuck on your finger. It happens often, but there are some really effective methods to remove a stuck ring. As long as you keep a level head, both you and the ring should escape unharmed.

BIRTHSTONES AND ENGAGEMENT RINGS

The concept of a birthstone rests on the notion that certain gems have a special affinity with specific months of the year. More importantly, these same gems have a special affinity to people who are born during the gem's month. It's a point of some contention where this idea comes from, but many researchers and historians trace it back to the Bible.

In Exodus, Moses lays out the description of a breastplate for his brother Aaron, who was by then the High Priest of the Hebrews. On this breastplate were set twelve precious stones, each emblazoned with the name of one of the twelve tribes of Israel. It's hard to know whether this is truly where birthstones started, but it's a largely accepted explanation.

Whatever their origin is, birthstones have been observed in many cultures around the world, and the lore around them seems to change often. Early practices involved wearing some piece of jewelry every month featuring the associated birthstone, but in the last few centuries, customs have shifted to wearing only one stone — the one we're born into.

Traditionally, different cultures chose their own birthstones based on certain beliefs, and these sets of birthstones had little to do with one another.

These days, birthstones have less to do with their historical origins. They are, in fact, so far removed that in 1912 the Jewelers of America (then called the National Association of Jewelers) had a meeting to agree on a standardized list of birthstones. This list was later updated and amended in 1952 and has since undergone minor changes in 2002 and 2016.

In Britain, the National Association of Goldsmiths would go on to create their own list of birthstones in 1937. Other cultures have complicated relationships between birthstones and celestial bodies which bestow certain benefits on individuals.

WHAT ELSE YOU SHOULD KNOW

This is all to say that there's no fully established and agreed-upon standard for which birthstone corresponds to which month. If this tradition holds any special meaning to you, you might consider purchasing an engagement ring with your future fiancée's birthstone either as the primary stone or as an accent stone. Even if you don't tend towards the lore associated with birthstones, it's interesting to know about the associated beliefs and where they come from.

Now, before jumping into the birthstones, there's something you should get acquainted with. By now, you've learned about many different types of grading criteria and measuring devices, but you might not be familiar with the Mohs hardness scale.

This scale was developed by the German geologist Friedrich Mohs and is used to determine how resistant a mineral is to scratching. The ten-point scale starts with talc at 1 — which can be scratched by a fingernail — and ends with diamond, which has a 10 rating. It's very useful for identifying minerals in the field and helps to get a rough idea of how easily a gem will become abraded in jewelry.

January Birthstone

January's birthstone is garnet. Garnets are mostly known for a deep red color and that's certainly the most common type of garnet. Other colors do occur, however, with varying degrees of frequency. Orange, brown, pink, yellow, and even green garnets have been found. The colors correspond to various minerals and metals that can be present as impurities in garnet. Uniquely among gemstones, garnets are magnetic — making them easy to identify from other similar stones with a strong magnet. Garnets are found all around the world and their value varies tremendously based on their quality and color.

The word garnet comes from the Latin granatus, which is associated with the word pomegranate. It's easy to see how this association was made considering garnet's similarity to the dark red pomegranate seeds. They were particularly popular among the nobility in medieval Europe.

The beauty of garnet is largely subjective; some people prefer the deep red of pyrope garnets while others like a lighter shade. When choosing a garnet, examine it closely under both natural and artificial light, because they tend to have inclusions that can create rather unpredictable effects in the gem.

Garnets make particularly beautiful cabochons (unfaceted gems), and the fact that they have no natural cleavage lines makes them good candidates for various cuts. They're quite hard (around 7.5 on Mohs hardness scale, placing them just under most emeralds), but they are prone to chipping or shattering. They're not a great choice for everyday wear, so they might not be appropriate on an engagement ring.

As a birthstone, garnets have numerous alleged powers and abilities. Chief among those is a calming aura. Garnets are said to help people become more peaceful, especially referring to inner peace and emotional stability. Garnets are believed to be particularly useful in times of crisis as they can be conducive to seeing things from a level-headed perspective without losing focus. In ancient times, they were also thought to help with diseases and "soothe an angry heart."

If you're a New Yorker, garnet is especially significant as the state gemstone of New York. Whether you're a believer in the powers of garnet or not, we could all use a little more peace and stability in our lives, so we might as well take whatever help is offered.

February Birthstone

Amethyst is February's gemstone, and they have captured our hearts and eyes for millennia with many examples appearing in royal

WHAT ELSE YOU SHOULD KNOW

collections all over the world — purple is thought to be the royal color, after all. This gem is a type of purple quartz, and it can be mined as well as grown in a lab. The rich purple hues of amethysts make them exceptionally attractive and a favorite of many people.

The name amethyst comes from a Greek word *amethystos*, which roughly translates to sober or sobriety. In ancient times, it was a widely held belief that amethysts would insulate their wearer from the effects of alcohol. There's little evidence to suggest that this theory is true, and we don't recommend that anyone put it to the test.

By extension, however, amethysts are thought to help keep a clear head, especially in battle and business affairs. Anyone engaged in our modern corporate battleground would find a steady, focused mind to be a great asset.

In most countries, but especially in the United States, the month of February is the least fecund — seeing the fewest births. If you're a February child, wear those amethysts with pride because you — like the gem — are unique and beautiful. Amethysts are also the gem of sixth wedding anniversaries, so they make a great gift to celebrate them.

Until around the mid-19th-century, amethysts were extremely rare, but discoveries in Brazil, Bolivia, and even some parts of the United States have made them much more common since then. The most highly-prized grade of amethyst is the so-called "deep Siberian," which is a deep purple color with slight red tones. However, many people find bolivianite, or ametrine to be the most stunning variety of amethyst. Ametrines are a blend of amethyst and citrine, forming a spectacular interplay between purple and yellow. The only naturally occurring source found so far is in Bolivia.

Amethysts are quite durable (7 on the Mohs scale) and can be used for daily wear, but they will require periodic repolishing. The gem is on the softer side compared to other gems, so it's susceptible to scratching if it comes into contact with diamonds, rubies, or emeralds. Heat, especially prolonged heat, can change the color of amethyst, so steam cleaning is not recommended.

Synthetic amethyst is very accessible and has all the properties of its natural counterpart. When buying amethyst jewelry, you're entitled to know if it's natural or synthetic. However, it's a relatively inexpensive gem and it won't make much difference for practical purposes.

Other birthstones traditionally associated with February have been hyacinth and pearl. Hyacinth (or jacinth) is a type of zirconia usually exhibiting red, orange, or yellow hues. Thoughts about jacinth's effects include strengthening of the heart and mind and accrual of wealth. It was also thought to be protective and featured on many talismans and amulets in the ancient world.

Pearls are quite familiar but don't typically make it on to rings, which is a shame because pearl rings can be very beautiful. They're referenced in religious texts of all the major religions and have been a part of human culture since it was recorded. Many cultural traditions continue to use pearls for various rituals to this day and they make a thoughtful gift. We'll talk more about pearls in June.

March Birthstone

March babies get to pick from two birthstones — aquamarine and bloodstone. These two couldn't be more different when it comes to their appearance. Aquamarine is the inspiration for the color of the same name and it gets its name from the Latin word for seawater. Bloodstones look a little more menacing and both their name and their color imply a sort of foreboding. Don't be dissuaded, though, as bloodstones can be stunning in the right setting.

Going by the zodiac, bloodstones are the true March gem. The typical bloodstone has a rich dark green hue interspersed with flecks of red. The characteristic red inclusions that give this gem its name are actually iron oxide trapped in the mineral. Like amethyst, bloodstone is also a type of quartz, but it's mostly found in the riverbeds of India, Brazil, and Australia.

In traditional lore, bloodstones were often associated with strength and health and were worn by athletes who believed it would improve their performance. More prized for their alleged abilities than their overt beauty, bloodstones are commonly used in amulets to preserve the wearer's good health and stamina.

The very fact that they are not so well known makes them stand out in the right piece of jewelry. The interplay between their dark and bright colors creates an eye-catching contrast. When choosing bloodstone jewelry, pick a gem that magnifies this contrast by looking for vivid red inclusions in deep green gems. They're particularly beautiful in a necklace or beaded bracelet. Unfortunately, most people find them unappetizing in engagement rings due to their imposing appearance.

The same standard of care should be given as with quartz stones. Bloodstone is a good candidate for cuts that feature a large table (the top facet of the gem), and if this is the case, it can make it susceptible to blows and impacts. Beads and cabochons are quite durable but will need to be re-polished periodically if they're frequently worn.

The other March gem — and the one that gets more attention — is aquamarine. Everything about this gem radiates peace and serenity. A variety of beryl, aquamarines are closely related to emeralds, but they're much more common. They are mined mostly in Brazil, but deposits have been discovered in various countries in Africa and the Middle East. The largest aquamarine formation ever found weighed a mind-boggling 242 pounds.

Generally, the more deeply saturated the stone is, the more valuable gems it will produce. The most highly prized color is the so-called Santa Maria blue, which beautifully displays the sparkle and beauty of aquamarines.

Sailors were historically very keen on aquamarines as it was believed that the gem would offer protection from rough waters. It's also believed that aquamarines help maintain a calm disposition, again making them attractive to sailors who often had to share living quarters for months on end.

More extreme superstitions called for wearing aquamarines as a cure for poisoning, though it's unclear how effective that proved to be. Less practical but more romantic bits of lore claim that the gem can reignite the passion and love between two people. This is probably why aquamarines are given on 19th wedding anniversaries. Mystical powers or not, aquamarines can serve as a splendid counterpoint in white gold or platinum jewelry.

When choosing an aquamarine, the primary and most important characteristic will be its color. Deeper shades of blue are more desirable and command the highest price. Different cuts will make a big difference with aquamarines, and larger fancy shape cuts tend to be the best at taking advantage of the light blue hues. Aquamarine can find a home in most settings, but solitaire settings or minimally accented ones are particularly suitable.

April Birthstone

April's gemstone needs no introduction given its prominent place in cultures around the world and in this very book. Those graced with an April birth have the good fortune of calling diamond their birthstone.

Diamonds get their name from the ancient Greek word adamas, meaning invincible or unconquerable. They have been traded as early as the 4th century BCE, mostly coming from India where they were found in various river basins. Today, diamonds are the traditional gem set in engagement rings, but throughout the centuries, their significance has changed markedly.

Diamonds have been associated with things ranging from warding off curses to being an aphrodisiac. Healing powers, curing the plague, and general good luck are only a few of the other powers that were attributed to diamonds at one time or another. The tumultuous history of diamonds has been at times as tragic as it has been uncanny.

The value of diamonds has seen a meteoric rise in the last century or so to the point that they are now the most valuable naturally occurring gems on earth. Much of diamonds' renown — and, by extension, their value — stems from their prominent role in pop culture. Slogans like "diamonds are forever" and "diamonds are a girl's best friend" didn't originate by accident. As a global culture, we're enthralled by diamonds to the point that it almost seems crass to choose any other stone for an engagement ring.

At this point, you probably know how tough and resilient diamonds are and how to tell a diamond's quality. For a refresher, remember the 4 Cs (clarity, cut, color, and carat weight) and pick diamonds whose cut serves to elevate their brilliance and character. They can, and will, easily scratch other gems they come into contact with, so they should always be stored separately and carefully.

Famous diamonds abound and it's difficult to choose one over another, but an easy contender for first place is the Great Star of Africa. The massive (530.2 carats) diamond was found in the Premier Mine in South Africa. It's now part of the Crown Jewels of the United Kingdom, mounted prominently in the Sovereign's Scepter.

Other notable examples are the Hope Diamond, whose legendary blue color was the inspiration for the fictional Heart of the Ocean, which was featured in the movie Titanic. Finally, perhaps the diamond that best portrays the sordid underbelly of the diamond trade is the highly controversial and disputed Koh-I-Noor diamond from India.

May Birthstone

The gem of spring, emerald, is the birthstone for those born in May. This gem has been highly prized for millennia — records exist of emerald mining in Egypt going back 2,500 years. Even Cleopatra valued them so immensely that she declared herself the owner of all the emerald mines of Egypt. They're often seen as a symbol of rebirth and evoke a sense of growth through their rich green hues.

The emerald gets its name from the Greek word *smaragdos*, which aptly translates to "green gem." Like the aquamarine, it's a variety of beryl mined in many parts of the world. As widespread as it is, Colombian emeralds tend to be the most valuable. Emeralds — alongside rubies, sapphires, and diamonds — are one of the four true precious stones. They're not graded like diamonds because emeralds tend to have many inclusions, but it is often the case that these inclusions add to their beauty.

They're evaluated on hue, tonal grade, and saturation by an expert's naked-eye viewing. Emeralds are often thought of as exclusively green, but they range in color from a golden yellow through to the deep viridian that they're most famous for.

For this reason, they're frequently treated to improve everything from their color to their surface appearance and inclusions. They're also typically cut in such a way that their integrity is not compromised, leading to the eponymous "emerald cut" — a long rectangular shape with straight parallel facets.

The alleged properties of emerald, as discussed previously, include an affinity for growth and rejuvenation, as well as loyalty and security. Emerald is said to both be a symbol of loyalty to another as well as evoke a sense of loyalty in that person. Historically, emeralds were also believed to hold various questionable medicinal properties.

The fact that a large percentage of emeralds undergo treatment for fracture filling or color corrective procedures makes untreated emeralds all the more valuable. When shopping for emerald jewelry, always make sure to ask if the emeralds have been treated or not and in what way.

There's nothing wrong with owning a treated emerald, but those stones should be kept away from heat sources and high pressures such as airplane cabins to avoid any potential damage.

Emeralds are quite appropriate in engagement rings and other jewelry for everyday wear. They rate between 7.5 and 8 on the Mohs scale, making them quite durable and resilient. However, they tend to have more cracks which can impact their durability. They're graded similarly to diamonds, but remember that color is everything for these stones — if the color is off, it will be a much less desirable emerald.

One of the largest and most famous emeralds is the uncut Duke of Devonshire Emerald. Gifted to the Duke of Devonshire by Pedro I of Brazil, it weighs over 1,300 carats and can be seen periodically on display at various museums in the United Kingdom.

Gargantuan stones aside, possibly the most well-known emeralds are the Bulgari stones that Elizabeth Taylor received from Richard Burton. That collection of emerald jewelry showcases some of the most stunning examples of the gem and proves that even diamonds sometimes pale in comparison.

June Birthstone

June is one of only three months to have not one or two but three different birthstones. Pearls, alexandrite, and moonstone are all available to those lucky enough to be born in June. These stones are all very different in appearance and value, so there's sure to be a perfect piece of jewelry out there for you.

Pearls have long been sought after jewels in human culture. The first records of pearls as precious jewels date back to 2300 BCE Mesopotamia. As most people know, pearls are made when an oyster or mussel coats an irritant within it with nacre over a long period of time. This makes pearls the only jewel that's made by a living organism. Pearls, and in particular natural saltwater pearls, hold a special place in the hearts of many people.

Natural South Sea pearls are the rarest and most valuable kind. For context, ten times more natural diamonds by weight are extracted each year than South Sea pearls. Color, luster, surface quality, and shape all play a role in the value of a pearl, and they're graded on a scale from AAA for the best quality pearls to A for poorest quality. Pearls aren't measured by carats but by size, and they typically range between three and thirteen millimeters.

Cultured pearls outnumber natural pearls by a very wide margin, and the odds are that any pearl you see in a jewelry store is a cultured one. Freewater pearl diving has become increasingly rare and cost-prohibitive to the point that it only happens in a handful of places on earth.

Freshwater mussels are fabulously productive when it comes to pearl farming — one mussel can produce up to 50 pearls at a time. In addition to their use in jewelry, many Asian cultures see powdered pearl as a remedy for a number of maladies, creating a steady demand.

Purity, longevity, and humility are all associated with pearls as a birthstone. The pearl necklace is a traditional setting in which the jewels are seen. Pearl engagement rings are uncommon but not unheard of. They can look very impressive in the right setting, but they're quite a bit softer than other gems and will require special care.

Keep in mind that pearls are very delicate; they reach a Mohs hardness of 2.5 at best. This makes them a poor choice for daily wear as they can scratch fairly easily.

Easily the most famous pearl is, ironically, one whose existence can't be confirmed at all. The pearl depicted by Johannes Vermeer in his *Girl with a Pearl Earring* has been a testament to the fascination with pearls that permeates through history.

In terms of tangible jewels, La Peregrina is the most famous pearl in the world. Throughout its 500-plus years of history, La Peregrina has been owned by African slaves, European royalty, and various wealthy merchants. Making a second appearance, Elizabeth Taylor ended up owning it, and the pearl was most recently sold at an auction for over eleven million dollars.

The second of the June gems is alexandrite. Alexandrites are quite rare and thereby quite valuable. The first significant deposits were found in the Ural Mountains of Russia, but those have long been mined out. Today, it's mostly found in Brazil, Sri Lanka, and some parts of Africa.

Although the story has not been confirmed, alexandrite reportedly got its name after Tzar Alexander II of Russia. It was named by a Finnish geologist prospecting for emeralds in the Urals. Those first Russian alexandrites were of far greater quality than the ones mined today, and they are now mostly found in museums and private collections.

The distinguishing characteristic of alexandrite is that it appears to change colors under different lighting conditions. In daylight, alexandrite appears green to light green, while under incandescent lighting it's a deep plum to red color. This color-changing property is not unique to alexandrite, but no other gem displays such a stark contrast between its visible hues.

They're graded on the 4 Cs — much like diamonds — but for alexandrites, color carries much more weight than the other Cs. The gem's chameleonic ability is so prized and captivating that it has been named the "alexandrite effect."

Alexandrite is mostly associated with learning and mental acuity, purportedly helping memory and information retention for those who wear them. They're also associated with love and romance, making them a good choice for engagement rings. It's a very tough gem (8.5), appropriate for everyday wear, and it makes a terrific primary stone with a diamond halo.

If you're in the market for an alexandrite, know that they can get quite expensive — even more so than diamonds in some cases. The primary trait you want to look for is a beautiful color, and don't forget to ask about any treatment. Fracture filling is not uncommon in alexandrites, and you should know if it has been performed.

The third and final gem for June babies is moonstone. Roman naturalist Pliny the Elder claimed that the color and appearance of moonstones changed with the phases of the moon. This led to them being associated with various Greek and Roman lunar gods and thereby becoming known as moonstones. In Indian religious lore, they were thought to be moonbeams solidified on earth.

Moonstone is a type of feldspar which displays overlapping microscopic layers. When these layers are at, or near, the wavelength of light, they cause light to scatter. This phenomenon and the associated milky luster of moonstones is called adularescence. A moonstone's adularescence is paramount when determining its value.

The ideal moonstone presents a bluish sheen with a completely colorless background. Gems with these traits were found almost exclusively in Sri Lanka, but they have, at least for the moment, become extremely scarce, causing their price to shoot up. There are other colors of moonstone, such as a light ochre and even pink and green, but the most common moonstones are grayish and highly lustrous.

By way of their association with lunar deities, moonstones are believed to have ties to healing and nourishing properties as well as other feminine energies.

These stones are typically seen in cabochon cuts which serve to best reveal their adularescence but also make them somewhat susceptible to damage. They're on the softer side and therefore not great for everyday wear. High heat can also cause damage to feldspar, so steam cleaning should be avoided.

WHAT ELSE YOU SHOULD KNOW

Moonstones can be a good choice for an engagement ring, but it's often hard to find a high-quality stone in the right setting. They were, however, quite popular with big-name designers of the Art Nouveau period, so some beautiful rings are out there if you're willing to put in the effort to find them.

July Birthstone

Those born in July have the honor of calling ruby their birthstone. The name ruby comes from the Latin *ruber*, meaning red. Rubies are second only to diamonds both in value and in most people's perceptions. In some parts of the world, they're much more highly prized than diamonds and have been culturally significant for thousands of years.

So revered were these gems that in ancient Sanskrit they were known as the "king of precious gems." To this day, rubies evoke a sense of awe and wonder, and seeing a natural high-quality ruby is a revelation for most people.

When they hear ruby, most people immediately summon the image of a deep crimson gem, and this red color is ruby's trademark. In fact, ruby is a variety of corundum which occurs in a very wide array of colors. What makes a ruby a ruby is its red color. The most desirable hue is a deep red with hints of purple called Pigeon's Blood.

Pigeon's Blood rubies were — and continue to be, albeit to a lesser extent — found in Myanmar's Mogok Valley, but extraction there has slowed. Deposits exist in many places of the world, including North and South America as well as Africa and India, but none of these have matched the quality of Southeast Asian rubies.

Their color has always drawn obvious comparisons to blood, leading people to associate rubies with health, vitality, and the heart. They're also seen as conducive to passion and love for the same reason. In medieval Europe, rubies were thought to generate wealth and prosperity for their owner, and it's easy to see why — anyone who was wealthy enough to own rubies was likely to become even wealthier.

In terms of toughness, rubies are almost as durable as diamonds (9 on the Mohs scale). They're perfectly appropriate for everyday use and won't suffer any damage with even a small amount of care. Rubies in engagement rings are not as common as diamonds but still quite typical. Many couples prefer them to diamonds because of their associations with love.

When purchasing a ruby, color is going to be the biggest factor in determining value. Rubies frequently undergo heat treatment to improve their color which doesn't impact their integrity at all. Other treatments, however, can make a difference. Fissure treatment to improve clarity can make them more prone to damage, so always get a full report of any treatments performed on a ruby before it's purchased.

Along with being the July birthstone, ruby is also the gem traditionally given at 15th and 40th wedding anniversaries. If you're fortunate enough to make it to 40 years of marriage, a ruby is the least you can do to mark the occasion.

Perhaps the most famous ruby out there is the Liberty Bell Ruby, a mammoth 8,500 carat stone that was sculpted into a miniature replica of the Liberty Bell studded with fifty diamonds. It's not quite what most people would consider gem-quality ruby as it's a very dark shade of red, but it's still quite impressive.

The most expensive ruby — and consequently the most expensive colored gemstone — to date is the Sunrise Ruby. It was originally mined in Myanmar and weighs just under 26 carats. The stone's color is near-perfect and it was mounted by the House of Cartier on a gold ring flanked by two diamonds. It has reached a top price of $30.4 million dollars at auction. The Sunrise Ruby is truly a sight to behold and has been named a "unique treasure of nature" by the Swiss Gemological Institute.

WHAT ELSE YOU SHOULD KNOW

August Birthstone

August is another month that has the distinction of having three birthstones. Peridot, sardonyx, and spinel are all August stones. They're quite different both in composition and color, and although sardonyx is the traditional birthstone for the month, nowadays peridot has become the frontrunner.

The mineral olivine is one of the few that produces gem-quality stones that don't owe their color to impurities but rather the structure of the mineral itself. Those high-quality stones are called peridots. It has been mined for thousands of years and it was frequently confused with topaz. In fact, the earliest recorded source of peridot is the Greek island of Topazios (which gave its name to topaz).

Peridot's etymology is a bit fuzzy and contentious, but experts largely agree that the most likely source is the word faridat — Arabic for "gem."

Peridot doesn't occur in very many colors; it's mostly an olive green to yellowish-green. Some variations do occur, but they're very rarely of gem-quality. Olivine is also quite soft and easy to break, so anything under one carat is usually not appropriate for faceting.

Nowadays, most of the world's supply of peridot comes from Arizona. Other significant deposits exist in Myanmar, Vietnam, China, and Pakistan. Myanmar in particular is very well known for its outstanding quality peridot.

The metaphysical qualities that the August birthstone is associated with are actually relatively broad. Peridot is thought to convey protection from evil in general and brings prosperity and good fortune. It's also been said to reduce envy, jealousy, and stress.

Peridots are not terribly expensive and can easily find a home on an engagement ring, especially as accent stones. When purchasing peridot, color is king — the greener the better. Ideally, you'll find a gem with no traces of yellow or brown. As mentioned earlier, it's not terribly durable, so it should be treated gently when cleaning. It's not exactly prone to chips and cracks, but it's softer than, say, topaz. Peridot is also the gem gifted on 16th wedding anniversaries.

Spinel is the second of the August birthstones. Their most striking attribute is how diverse and versatile they are. They have been found in a very wide variety of colors, and their hardness makes them vastly popular in jewelry. Spinel gets its name from the Latin word *spina*, meaning arrow or thorn. This probably has to do with its octahedral structure that resembles an arrowhead.

The many colors of spinel have caused it to be mistaken throughout history for many other gems. Rubies, in particular, were susceptible to this confusion to the point that the most famous ruby in the world was discovered to be a spinel upon closer examination. This was the Black Prince Ruby, which is mounted on the Imperial State Crown of England. Such is the resemblance that even the most experienced jewelers were fooled for hundreds of years.

This birthstone is found in many parts of the world and color can be a good indication of provenance. Blue and pink spinels are found in parts of Sri Lanka. A deep red spinel and red with violet tones is mined in Vietnam. An orangish-red variety is found in Tanzania. Many other sources of spinel exist with more or less characteristic color patterns. The most valuable spinels are those that best mimic their extravagant red cousins.

Their frequent red coloring gave them a reputation for relieving blood-related illnesses and inflammation. Other superstitions are their ability to soothe flaring tempers and promote general well-being.

Spinels are a decent choice for engagement rings, either as a center stone or accent stones. The paler a spinel is, typically the less valuable it will be. For higher quality spinels, look for intense colors — red in particular. Gems with little to no inclusions should be selected as the inclusions can have a significant impact on appearance in spinels.

They often undergo various types of treatment, so be sure to ask about what has been done to the gem. Exposure to high heat has a tendency to reduce the intensity of the gems, which makes steam cleaning a bad idea.

Last, but certainly not least, is sardonyx. This birthstone is appropriately named by combining its two component minerals — sard and onyx. Both of these are varieties of chalcedony and under the right circumstances can form a beautiful layered effect. It's one of the most ancient of the birthstones, and it's believed that sardonyx was one of the original stones on Aaron's breastplate. The ideal sardonyx has reddish-orange stripes interrupted by white ones.

Both sard and onyx can range in color from yellowish-brown to a deep rust color. This is appropriate because it's actually the presence of iron oxide that bestows that color in them. The most valuable sardonyx gems are those that display the stark contrast between their layers.

Since ancient times, sardonyx was prized for use in signets and seals. Its velvety texture is ideal for carving seals because it prevents wax from sticking to them. It was also a very popular stone for cameos. In fact, to this day, sardonyx cameos are still being produced. Their wide distribution all over Europe turned them into a mainstay throughout medieval times, especially for their purported abilities to instill courage and happiness.

The most valuable and attractive sardonyx has historically been sourced from India. Deposits in other parts of the world, such as Brazil and other American nations, are quite promising, and a lot of great sardonyx has been mined there.

Both sard and onyx are relatively hard and can be used in rings but may not be ideal for everyday wear. They're prone to fissures if mistreated and are frequently treated or dyed. Traditionally, sardonyx isn't desirable as a primary stone in an engagement ring. When buying sardonyx jewelry, it's important to get a certified analysis because imitations do exist. For purposes of cleaning and care, it can be treated the same as peridot.

September Birthstone

In September, we find the last of the true precious stones — the sapphire. This gem certainly has a rich history, often making appearances in the ancient world. The name sapphire comes from an Ancient Greek word *sáppheiros*, which was probably used to denote lapis lazuli (a semi-precious stone), but there are indications that it may have even older origins in Sanskrit. It's a variety of corundum, like ruby.

In fact, ruby is the only variety of corundum that isn't called sapphire. Various impurities make corundum appear in different colors, but only red corundum is called ruby. Nevertheless, most people associate the word sapphire with a rich blue color. The color is caused by the presence of titanium and iron in various degrees within the stone. Generally speaking, the value of sapphires is mostly tied to the quality of their blue color.

Most sapphire today is mined in Madagascar, but many places in the world have been major producers in the past. China, Australia, and Sri Lanka have seen their fair share of high-quality sapphires. The Kashmir sapphires of the Zanskar mountain range constitute a special instance.

For a long time during the 19th and 20th centuries, the Kashmir region produced some of the most valuable sapphires in the world. The sapphires are largely depleted today but examples remain which are spectacularly valuable. The sapphires from the region have a velvety blue color and texture that makes them exceptionally desirable.

Throughout history, the September birthstone has fascinated nobility and high-class society. Its associations with romance, fidelity, and mystery have given it an almost mystical status. They're not only the September birthstone; they're also given on the 5th and 45th wedding anniversary. Greeks also believed that sapphire would protect its wearer from harm and envy, and anyone wearing a gorgeous sapphire certainly has little to envy.

Sapphires have always been a reasonable alternative to diamonds in engagement rings. They're close to the same hardness and resilience, so they're perfectly acceptable for everyday wear and are typically more affordable. Vintage engagement rings are especially good settings for sapphires and they can be found quite often.

Sapphire's value is tied very closely to its color, so they're frequently heat-treated to improve their color and clarity. Any treatments should be disclosed when you buy a sapphire. A very popular design is the three-stone sapphire set in a platinum or white gold band.

Throughout history, there have been many famous and infamous sapphires but perhaps none so much as the sapphire engagement ring owned by Kate Middleton. The British Royal family has long held a fascination with sapphires and it's that same ring that Princess Diana received from Prince Charles.

Another famous sapphire, The Blue Giant of the orient, is the largest faceted sapphire in the world — weighing 486.52 carats. It was mined in Sri Lanka and sold to an anonymous collector in 1907, and has by all accounts disappeared from public view. As mysteriously as it had vanished, the gem found its way to an auction in 2004 and was eventually sold for a million dollars.

October Birthstone

October babies have two options to choose from — opal and tourmaline. Opals have been the October birthstone for hundreds of years and evidence of opal mining exists in North America dating back as early as 10,000 BCE. The most likely etymology for opal is that it got its name from the Sanskrit word úpala.

Opal is very different from most other gems in that it is amorphous. In gemological terms, that means that it doesn't have a crystal structure. Rather, it's composed of many small silica spheres that reflect light in different ways based on their size. This peculiar structure gives opal its most salient attribute — its play-of-light.

This play-of-light, or opalescence, fascinated ancient people, and Romans considered it to be the most precious of all gems. So cherished were opals back then that the Roman Senator Nonius chose exile over the sale of his prized opal to Emperor Marcus Antonius. William Shakespeare referred to opal as the "Queen of Gems" and to this day it continues to be a favorite of many people.

The famous home of opals is Australia. Since the discovery of vast deposits in the 1880s, Australia has produced well over 90% of the world's supply of opals. Other notable deposits have since been discovered in Ethiopia, which may rival Australia's, and other parts of the world continue to produce relatively smaller quantities.

In broad terms, opal is classified as either precious or common. Common opal doesn't display the opalescence typical of the stone, while precious opal does. It doesn't correlate to the value of the stone directly, but generally speaking, common opal tends to be less expensive.

However, those two categories divide into a multitude of different types of opal. Some of the notable kinds are black opal, fire opal, white opal, Madagascar's girasol opals, and many more. They're usually classified in accordance with their background, which is to say the parts of the stone that aren't silica.

The value of opals is closely tied to their availability. The right black opal, for instance, can reach prices of several hundred dollars per carat. The much more common white opal of Coober Pedy, Australia is much more affordable.

WHAT ELSE YOU SHOULD KNOW

Opals are quite soft and should be handled with care. Many other precious stones will scratch their surface, reducing their opalescence significantly. There are so many varieties of opal that it's really up to you if you think it belongs on an engagement ring.

The cut most conducive to display an opal's beauty is the cabochon and most gem-quality opals are cut this way. It can make a good center stone, but it requires some extra care, and extreme conditions of any kind should be avoided (e.g. high temperature, high pressure, etc.).

Many opals have made headlines throughout history and the most famous of those is the Olympic Australis. Weighing an incredible 17,000 carats, Australis is the largest opal ever found. It was discovered in 1956 and got its name from the Olympic Games happening at the time in Melbourne. It's currently valued at just under two million dollars.

Tourmaline, the other October birthstone, is renowned for the variety of colors that it displays. The name stems from the Sinhalese words *tura mali*, which roughly translate to "stone of many colors." Tourmaline's rainbow spectrum stems from the fact that tourmaline is actually a family of minerals rather than a single type of gem.

The difference in chemical composition gives rise to different names for tourmalines based on their color. Rubellite is the vibrant red variant, indicolite tends towards green and blue hues, verdelite has deep green tones, and so on. Black tourmaline — also called schorl — was very popular in the middle ages, but is very rarely seen nowadays. All the colors of tourmaline result from various trace minerals in the stones, and the most desirable colors have been found in Brazil in what is called Paraiba tourmaline after the area where it was found.

It's fitting that the most diverse and varied stone was selected to be the national gemstone of the United States. Several important deposits were active in the US, especially in Maine and California. Empress Dowager Cixi of China had such a penchant for this multicolored stone that she almost single-handedly propped up the tourmaline trade in California until her death in 1908.

Paraiba tourmaline is some of the most impressive, exhibiting bright and almost neon-like colors. It's largely exhausted in Brazil, but some promising discoveries have been found in parts of Africa that yield similar stones.

In addition to being an October birthstone, it's also the gem of 8th wedding anniversaries. Properties are attributed to tourmaline in relation to its color. Black tourmaline has been thought to provide strong protection from ill will, while pink and red tourmalines evoke love and passion. Stamina, good health, and strength have all been associated with green tourmaline. The history of tourmaline is riddled with egregious cases of mistaken identity. In the 1500s, Spanish conquistadors mistook tourmaline for emerald, and the notion persisted almost 300 years until tourmaline was classified as a different gem. More recently, one of the Russian imperial jewels — the Caesar's Ruby pendant — which was long thought to be a ruby, was determined to be a red tourmaline.

Tourmaline sits comfortably around 7.5 on the Mohs hardness scale, making it appropriate for everyday jewelry. Color is, once again, the name of the game; pink and deep red tourmalines are the most desirable, followed closely by greenish-blue. It's sometimes treated to improve clarity and/or color which greatly reduces the value, so you should know if treatments were performed on any gem you're considering purchasing.

High-quality tourmaline of over one carat is rare, but it will usually be more affordable than a diamond engagement ring. Ultrasonic and steam cleaning aren't recommended, especially for treated stones.

WHAT ELSE YOU SHOULD KNOW

November Birthstone

November is another dual birthstone month. Topaz and citrine are the November birthstones and they're actually quite similar. Similar enough, in fact, that they have been frequently mistaken for one another. Topaz makes an appearance in many ancient texts, including the Bible and Greek naturalist treatises, but it's not clear that the topazes discussed there were true topaz given their similarity to other gems.

For a long time, any gem that was yellow was thought to be topaz. Modern mineral assessments were able to separate topaz into its own type of mineral, but mistakes still occur. The name topaz probably comes from the Greek island of Topazios (modern-day St. John's Island), but some sources claim its true origin is tapas, the Sanskrit word for fire. Whichever theory is correct doesn't change the fact that topaz continues to be a very popular stone.

Natural topaz stones are either colorless, light blue, or a vibrant yellow. The crystalline structure of topaz makes it a prime candidate for many kinds of treatment, making it available in a very wide array of colors. However, these treated topazes are worth a fraction of what their natural counterparts go for.

By far the most valuable variety of topaz is the so-called Imperial Topaz. These display a rich, golden color with pink and purple undertones. For a long time, their only source was Russia's Ural mountain range and the name is related to an imperial ban on owning them for anyone outside of the royalty.

Most topazes on the market are some shade of blue. It's almost a given that any blue topaz you see in a jewelry store will have been treated to improve or change its color. The three varieties of blue topaz are sky blue, Swiss blue, and London blue, and they span the gamut of hues from lightest to darkest.

Topaz deposits are abundant all over the world. Brazil is the most important producer of gem-quality topaz, but other sources include Pakistan, Russia, and Australia. It has been discovered as far afield as Sri Lanka and Madagascar. This makes topaz quite common and relatively inexpensive on the whole. Don't be fooled, though, a very high-end natural imperial topaz can easily be much more expensive than even diamonds.

The many properties assigned to topaz have changed throughout history, but Greeks prized it mostly for its purported ability to increase strength and vitality. In India, wearing topaz jewelry is thought to increase longevity and intelligence, and medieval Europeans believed it had strong anti-magic properties.

Blue topaz, natural or otherwise, is the 4th wedding anniversary stone, while imperial topaz is given on the 23rd wedding anniversary. Colorless topaz has become a very viable alternative to diamonds in engagement rings as a placeholder. Their similar appearance and hardness make them fairly indiscernible to the untrained eye. Even though topaz is very hard (8 on the Mohs scale), it is not overly tough. It can chip easily and should thus be handled with care.

There is a special kind of this gem called mystic topaz. These aren't natural stones but are instead the result of a process which coats a colorless topaz with a titanium film. The process results in a gem with a vibrant rainbow sparkle. Mystic topazes need a little extra care. Although the coating is permanent, it can be removed by buffing or overly rough conditions.

The structure of this birthstone is such that it lends itself to very large formations. Larger gems are fairly easy to come by, and the largest faceted gem in the world is a topaz. The El-Dorado Topaz found in Brazil weighs a jaw-dropping 31,000 carats — and that's after 80% of its weight was lost in processing. It's hard to estimate its value, but it's certainly in the millions of dollars. Citrine is the second gem of November babies and it's very commonly mistaken for topaz. It's actually almost impossible to visually distinguish similar shades of topaz and citrine. Citrines range from a bright yellow to a brownish yellow color and they're very abundant worldwide. The name citrine probably comes from the French word for lemon, *citron*.

A type of quartz, citrine is found just about everywhere amethyst is present. So closely related are they that they can sometimes occur on the same stone, as discussed previously, in the gem ametrine.In the mid-18th century, a procedure was devised to heat treat amethysts, which changed their color to yellow. This treatment of amethyst and smoky quartz produces the vast majority of citrine available on the market today. Naturally occurring citrine is actually quite rare. The heat treatment is very stable and the color will not pale over time.

Perhaps due to its golden hues, citrine has been prized throughout history for its ability to promote wealth and prosperity. Greek and Roman senators were especially fond of citrine rings and had citrine carved into various shapes.

With a rating of 7 on the Mohs scale (like most quartz), it's a good choice for jewelry. The fact that it doesn't exhibit cleavage along with its abundance makes citrine perfect for fancy cuts and bespoke jewelry. It won't require too much extra care, but harder gems such as diamonds and topazes will scratch it. Given that it's very likely to be heat-treated, citrine should be kept away from high temperatures, and steam cleaning is not recommended.

The relative accessibility of even large citrines means that carat weight will not exponentially influence its value. Even larger gems will be reasonably priced. However, given how easy it is to produce treated citrine, you should always buy from a reputable jeweler if you're in the market for natural stones.

December Birthstone

Finally, December is another triple month featuring the lovely tanzanite, zircon, and turquoise birthstones. They're all blue (though zircon comes in many colors), so if you or your loved one is a fan of the color, there's a lot to choose from. One of these is bound to accommodate any budget as well due to their wide range of quality options.

Tanzanite is a relative newcomer to the gem world. Discovered only in 1967, it was first assumed to be sapphire. Tanzanite only occurs naturally in the Merelani Hills of Tanzania from where it gets its name. Tanzanite is the blue variety of the mineral zoisite, and it naturally occurs mostly as a brownish or dull blue stone. Heat treating the gems alters the oxidative state of vanadium in the mineral, resulting in the rich blue tanzanite that is so prized. The heat treatment doesn't cause any stability issues.In the last few years, new tanzanite deposits have been found that yielded green gems. Some gems have even been found naturally displaying both green and blue hues in their makeup. These are extremely rare and tanzanite, in general, is exceedingly rare, much more so than diamonds. Cognac-colored stones have also been cropping up sporadically. Their color turns into a very light pinkish hue when heat treated.

Tiffany & Co. saw the potential in this gem and mounted an aggressive marketing campaign after securing distribution rights. Today, tanzanite extraction is still going strong. However, it is estimated that this pace will exhaust known supplies in as little as thirty years.

The first of the December birthstones rates between 6 and 7 on the Mohs scale, making it quite appropriate for jewelry. It isn't quite ideal for rings, however, especially rings that will be frequently worn. Tanzanite makes a great substitute for sapphire.

Although it isn't quite as eye-catching as the highest quality sapphire, tanzanite's velvety color can often be more attractive in the right

WHAT ELSE YOU SHOULD KNOW

setting. The price of tanzanite is known to fluctuate quite a bit, so it's best to only buy from highly reputable sources.

In no particular order, the second gem of December is turquoise. Unlike tanzanite, turquoise has been known as a precious stone for thousands of years. Torquoise is a phosphate mineral that ranges from blue to green shades and has a waxy sheen. The earliest known mining of turquoise took place around 3000 BCE in the Sinai Peninsula, but its history is older than that, with some pieces of jewelry dating to almost 5000 BCE.

Ancient Egyptians were fascinated by the stone, and it was present in all the major civilizations of the ancient world. Mesoamerican civilizations used it in jewelry, it was used in rituals by native North Americans, and it has even been seen in Mesopotamian jewelry. King Tutankhamen's mask is inlaid partially with turquoise. It was believed to provide strength and strong protection against everything from physical attacks to magical curses.

One of the oldest sources of the stone are mines in Iran, which used to produce the finest turquoise. When the stone made it to Europe in the 13th century, it was via Turkey. This led many to conclude that it was mined there, when in fact it was coming from modern-day Iran. This confusion led to turquoise being named *pierre tourques*, French for Turkish stone, from where it gets the name.

Unfortunately, modern imitations and treatments have greatly reduced the value of turquoise. Treating stones with wax or oil is a generally accepted practice, especially on high-quality stones. However, procedures such as dyeing and stabilization — where a resin is used to create a better surface appearance — alter the stone significantly. Turquoise is even used in a process called reconstitution, wherein small fragments of stone are powdered and mixed into a resin matrix to produce convincing imitations.

It's quite a delicate stone, relatively hard but susceptible to chemicals and light. Even cosmetics or perspiration will affect its coloration over time. This makes it poorly suited for everyday wear, but lovely for special occasions. Cabochons and beads are the most desirable cuts for turquoise.

It should be kept away from high temperatures, especially if treated with waxes or oils. When buying turquoise, you'll have to rely on the reputation of the jeweler, because it's difficult to determine which treatments have been applied to these stones.

The third of December's birthstones is zircon. When most people hear zircon, they think cubic zirconia (CZ), which is a manmade diamond simulant. These are distinct from zircon, which is a naturally occurring stone. Zircon is the common name of zirconium silicate, the oldest gemstone on earth; in fact, it is the oldest known substance on earth.

Zircons have been found that formed around the same time as the Earth itself. It has been mined extensively throughout history and, given its various colors, is one of the doppelganger stones commonly mistaken for several others. Colorless zircon of fine gem quality rivals diamond in terms of brilliance and fire, and it passed for diamond before modern assessment methods were developed.

The origin of the name zircon is debated, but it lies in either the Arabic word *zarkun* or the Persian *zargun*. Either way, zircon mining has not declined since ancient times. Today, the majority of the world's zircon comes from Australia.

Jack Hills in Australia is an area so renowned for the zircon extracted there that it's sometimes referred to as Zircon Hills. Other significant sources exist in Sri Lanka, Tanzania, Myanmar, and Cambodia. Conveniently, each area produces a slightly different color of zircon as different impurities were present during their formation.

Blue zircon, specifically, is the birthstone variety. Blue zircon was believed to have the ability to ward off evil spirits as well as induce sleep. Other properties often seen were the potential to increase prosperity and improve wisdom.

Most zircon extracted nowadays is heat treated to improve its color. The heat treatment is relatively stable, but long exposure to bright light has been known to revert it closer to its original shade. It's a very suitable substitute for diamonds in engagement rings, but it's somewhat softer (7 to 7.5 on the Mohs scale). You should also take into account that it's quite dense and will appear smaller than some other gems of the same weight. Zircon abrades much more easily than diamonds, so extra care should be taken when undertaking activities that may expose it to impacts. It's graded on the same system as diamonds and usually cut in a way to best display its brilliance. The misconceptions surrounding this underrated gem make it relatively inexpensive. Whether it's a birthday gift or an engagement ring, zircon is a great choice.

CZ RING VS. DIAMOND RING

A lot has been said about diamonds, and they have become something of a hot-button issue in recent years. Broadly speaking, there are two camps. On one side are people who consider a diamond to be just another mineral, useful for its properties but certainly not worth what jewelers sell them for. The other side believes that diamonds are intrinsically beautiful and that their beauty and rarity make them valuable.

The issue isn't whether one side is right or wrong; it's about the question that each is trying to answer. That question is: what matters when gifting diamonds, the intention or the action?

If you think the action of buying an engagement ring serves to formally conclude a proposal and eventually move on to the next symbolic step — marriage — then you probably don't buy into the hype of diamonds. If, however, you believe that there's more to an engagement than a transactional agreement and you want to communicate your love, not only to your girlfriend but also to the people in your life, then you'll accept no substitutes.

Cubic zirconia was touched on in the previous section, but it deserves a closer look. As discussed, this is a lab-grown gem that resembles a diamond. To be fair, its appearance is very close to a natural diamond with a few important exceptions.

The most important difference between CZ and diamond is the price. As a manufactured gem, CZ is both more common (millions of carats are made each year) and cheaper than diamond. This price difference is significant, and for people who just can't afford a diamond at that point in their lives, it's a decent substitute.

One of the issues that some people have with CZ is, paradoxically, its impeccable clarity. CZs are always flawless, lacking even the slightest inclusion or blemish. This property makes them a little boring. Even though their brilliance and fire are similar to those of diamonds, they look a bit lifeless as there's nothing there to break up the sparkle.

Additionally, CZ is quite a bit softer than diamond. It rates between 8 and 8.5 on the Mohs hardness scale. That may seem pretty close to diamond's 10, but the Mohs scale isn't linear and the difference is actually quite significant. The upshot is that CZ will become cloudy after prolonged periods of use and will either have to be replaced or re-polished.

The one aspect in which CZ outperforms diamond is its color availability. The nature of the zirconium dioxide crystal is such that it can have elements added in the formation to alter its color in a process known as doping. Doped gems can have just about any color you can imagine and even an assortment of colors on the same stone.

If you want a fancy-colored gem and you just can't find the right diamond, CZ is a good alternative. In this case, the price difference is even starker. Fancy-colored diamonds can be remarkably expensive, while the price for colored CZs are practically the same as for colorless.

WHAT ELSE YOU SHOULD KNOW

Ultimately, if price is your primary concern, you should consider CZ. It's not the same, and it won't have the brilliance and depth of a natural diamond, but nothing should stand between you and the one you love.

There is one more recent addition to this debate, and that's moissanite. Introduced in commercial quantities only recently, moissanite is a nearly colorless gem that closely resembles a diamond. It's composed of silicon carbide and very rarely occurs naturally, so all moissanite on the market (for practical purposes) is synthetic.

Moissanite is much closer in hardness to diamond (9.25 on the Mohs scale) and has facets that are just as attractive as those on a diamond. It's much more expensive than CZ but still considerably cheaper than diamond. It can be seen as a sort of middle ground between the two in a lot of aspects.

Moissanite production hasn't been completely perfected. Most stones retain a very slight yellowish tint, but it's almost imperceptible. Another drawback is that it exhibits double refraction where light rays are divided into two separate rays when hitting it, which is detrimental to the brilliance when viewed closely.

Moissanites are gems in themselves and should be thought of as such. They may look like diamonds, but they're certainly not diamonds. The fact is that not every occasion is going to call for diamonds, and moissanites make wonderful gifts for many such occasions. However, an engagement (especially the first engagement) is not just any occasion, and it should be marked by something special.

As you can see, there are some options to choose from if you object to diamonds ethically or based on price. CZ and moissanite are guaranteed to be conflict-free and most certainly cheaper, but there's really no substitute for a natural diamond in an engagement ring.

SECOND MARRIAGE ETIQUETTE

No one ever enters a marriage with the intent of divorcing. Marriage is about great expectations and a belief that some things in life do last forever. Unfortunately, that doesn't always work out. It actually doesn't work out quite often, as the percentage of first marriages that result in divorce is rising.

This doesn't mean that marriage is inherently an outdated concept. It just means that the right person hasn't come along. A second marriage doesn't have to be any less important just because you've been through it all before. In fact, treating a second marriage with as much importance as your first — and in some cases more — is a key factor for its success.

There are no real guidelines that need to be followed in terms of the proposal that are any different from the first time. There's nothing immature about going all out and planning a big proposal for your second marriage, either. Most women will appreciate the effort, especially if they also have one marriage behind them but didn't have a grandiose proposal the first time around.

In a way, you should think about your second marriage as a chance to outdo yourself in every way and make sure that it lasts for the rest of your life. If you're lucky, you will have learned from your mistakes and will be ready to embark on this journey; you will certainly be a little older, but hopefully a little wiser too.

In terms of the engagement ring, see it as an opportunity to think outside the box. A diamond solitaire is still a great choice, but you can probably be a little bolder. Maybe you'd like to shirk tradition and choose colored stones or select an ornate, vintage-style ring. Again, there are no real rules, and that goes both ways — you can be as conservative or as opulent as you feel is right. Understand that tastes change and people may want to distance themselves from their previ-

WHAT ELSE YOU SHOULD KNOW

ous lifestyle in their choice of jewelry, so if this is her second marriage, don't try to find a ring that matches her previous engagement ring.

Another benefit you'll have is that you've navigated the whole ring-buying rigamarole once before. You're probably much more knowledgeable about stone quality, metal options, and the rest of the factors involved. This will allow you to make a more educated decision and probably avoid some of the pitfalls of choosing a ring.

Wearing an engagement ring or wedding band from a previous marriage after a second engagement is not a good idea. Even if your partner is outwardly tolerant, it sends the wrong signals. Some people choose to ignore this in favor of honoring a lost spouse, but it should be discussed as a couple. A second marriage is often a chance to get things right and holding on to the past can only get in the way of that. Some people even choose to restyle their first ring or use the materials to have a new one made.

Some people find it a little easier to plan a second engagement jointly. At the very least, marriage should be well discussed ahead of time. It does remove the surprise element, but the merit of a surprise may be overshadowed by the need to be a little more pragmatic at that point in your life. Let your personal circumstances guide your decisions. However, everybody loves a surprise, and a surprise proposal will mean just as much the second time as it did the first.

One thing that you definitely shouldn't do is ask for the engagement ring from your first marriage back. First and foremost, it's in extremely poor taste. Second, engagement rings are generally regarded as a gift that cannot be revoked (especially if the marriage takes place), and you probably don't have any claim to ownership. In special cases, such as the ring being a family heirloom, this can turn into a difficult situation. You'll need to be very diplomatic and try to reach some sort of common-sense understanding with your previous spouse if the ring has enormous sentimental value.

Another thing that's very important is to make sure that any previous marriage is fully annulled before the engagement. Married people can propose and become engaged, but it's far less complicated — both emotionally and legally — to completely finalize a divorce before doing so.

Overall, not a great deal changes for the second engagement. You should still buy a ring, and that ring should still be as beautiful as you can manage. There's maybe a little more leeway about making a big surprise proposal, but the value of grand gestures should never be underestimated.

HOW TO REMOVE A RING THAT IS STUCK

If you find yourself looking at your ring finger one day and thinking "was that always so tight," you're not alone. Getting a ring stuck on a finger is a fairly common scenario. It's quite normal, particularly for people who don't take their ring off for extended periods.

First and foremost, there's no reason to panic. You'll rarely — if ever — be in a situation where taking the ring off immediately is of vital importance. Calmly take stock of the situation and go over the solutions outlined here to find the one that best suits you. Don't reach for those bolt cutters just yet, because there are many ways to get a stuck ring off that don't involve damaging it.

The most common cause for a ring becoming stuck is water retention. When the body retains water, tissue will swell to accommodate it, and your fingers will become larger. Your first course of action is to expel some of that water and try to free up some space between the finger and the ring.

One of the causes of water retention is sodium in the body. For starters, spend a day drinking plenty of water to flush sodium out of your system. Overnight, the water will deplete, so the following

WHAT ELSE YOU SHOULD KNOW

morning is the time to act. Upon waking, place the hand in ice water elevated above the head. The ice water will constrict blood vessels, further reducing the size of the finger.

After about five minutes, pat the finger dry and apply any household lubricant. Vaseline works great, as does mineral oil or even cooking oil or grease. Wear a latex or neoprene glove to get a good grip on the ring when it's lubricated, and then try to remove it. All these factors combined should be enough to get the ring off.

If you're in a little more of a hurry, there's a quicker method that works fairly well but is more uncomfortable. Take a piece of string or floss about three feet long and slip it under the ring, leaving most of it towards the fingertip. Starting at the ring, wind the floss around your finger slowly until you reach just above the second knuckle of your ring finger.

Make sure its wound tightly to compress the finger but don't overdo it as you risk harming the finger. When it's done, tug on the floss from the other side of the ring, pulling towards the fingertip. This should slide the ring over the floss as it unwinds on the other side.

This second method is relatively fast and works great in a pinch. It can also be combined with the first for best results if circumstances allow. Anti-inflammatory creams can also be of assistance in reducing swelling in the finger.

Some combination of these tricks will probably be able to help get the ring off. However, in some cases, a medical condition will make it impossible or too painful to apply the kind of pressure necessary to remove a ring. If that happens, you may need to cut it.

Cutting a ring, especially one as valuable as an engagement ring, should be considered a last resort, but it doesn't have to be as bad as it sounds. It definitely shouldn't be a DIY operation as that can damage the ring much more than necessary. If removing the ring is a legitimate emergency, treat it as such and head to the nearest emergency room where it will be removed under the right conditions. If it's just stuck but there's no danger to your finger, most jewelers will be able to help you.

Every jeweler will have some kind of ring cutter and will know how to cut the ring in such a way as to minimize damage to it. If it doesn't require too much stretching to get it off, it may be able to get re-soldered without any lasting harm. Wherever the ring is cut, make sure you pay close attention to the stones. Stones can come loose in the process of removal, so make sure they're all accounted for.

This situation is a reason to never purchase a tungsten carbide or titanium engagement ring or wedding band. Those metals are extremely hard and therefore quite brittle. It's very likely that the ring will be completely destroyed if it ever needs to be removed by force. The recommended method for tungsten rings actually involves shattering the ring via concentric pressure.

So don't lose your cool if a ring gets stuck. There are quite a few ways that are overwhelmingly effective at getting it off, and some combination of them will probably solve your problem. When you do get a ring removed, it's a good idea to resize it when getting it repaired, or in case of pregnancy, stop wearing it for a while.

TIME TO PROPOSE

That about covers everything you need to know to execute the perfect engagement. At this point, you should feel more confident about your decision and ready to take the plunge. You can easily navigate ring styles and choose the one that's right for your special occasion based on her style. You know everything you need to say not only to her, but also her family and her friends. There's no shortage of proposal ideas for you to choose from and you know how to ask all the right questions when it comes to diamonds and other gemstones. All that's left is to go out there and do it!

As a parting thought, remember to cherish your future wife. Marriage is about a lot of things, both social and personal. Sure, there's a spectacular proposal that you planned to the finest detail, and then there are cakes, and flowers, and merrymaking, but all that falls away rather quickly. What you're left with in the end is the inelegant grunt work of building a life with another person — and not just a life that includes that person.

It's not enough, as Khalil Gibran so eloquently puts it, to "sing and dance together and be joyous, but let each one of you be alone." It's not enough to have a roommate that you can tolerate. A real, lasting bond requires that you give of yourself and expect your partner to give of themselves in return. When you're able to act together and place the needs of the family unit above your own, you'll be on the right track for a successful marriage.

That grunt work in the trenches of daily life is where marriage occurs and where its mettle is tested. Marriage is a commitment that you make every day, and if you hold back on that commitment or attempt to go halfway, you'll be in for a rough time. You'll find that the more you give, the more you get back, and a true union between two people can be the strongest source of strength.

We wish you all the love and success that you deserve.

ABOUT US

Michael Khordipour and Afshin Shaddaie founded Estate Diamond Jewelry in 1980. We started our company with a common love for rare and old jewelry.

We realized that there was a market of like-minded people who wanted something special and unique for their wedding proposal, and so we threw our energy into vintage and custom-made vintage-style rings.

Before long we became the world's top authority on vintage rings.

Collectors, celebrities and royalty began making appointments to view our collections at our 5th Avenue showroom. Our company began to generate media and international attention.

Recently, Michael's son Benjamin joined the company and Afshin and Benjamin decided that it was high time to put this book in motion.

Writing this book has taken almost a year, but it has been a wonderful experience.

We would love to hear how this book helped you. Please feel free to leave us a message. You can reach us at www.estatediamondjewelry.com/book

www.ingramcontent.com/pod-product-compliance
Lightning Source LLC
Chambersburg PA
CBHW050201130526
44591CB00034B/1655